KATE HEAP

SERIES EDITOR: EMMA TURNER

PRIMARY ENGLISH IN ACTION

IN ACTION SERIES

A **WALKTHRUs** PRODUCTION

hachette LEARNING

hachette LEARNING

www.hachettelearning.com

Together we unlock every learner's unique potential

At Hachette Learning (formerly Hodder Education), there's one thing we're certain about. No two students learn the same way. That's why our approach to teaching begins by recognising the needs of individuals first.

Our mission is to allow every learner to fulfil their unique potential by empowering those who teach them. From our expert teaching and learning resources to our digital educational tools that make learning easier and more accessible for all, we provide solutions designed to maximise the impact of learning for every teacher, parent and student.

Aligned to our parent company, Hachette Livre, founded in 1826, we pride ourselves on being a learning solutions provider with a global footprint.

To order, please visit www.HachetteLearning.com or contact Customer Service at education@hachette.co.uk / +44 (0)1235 827827.

ISBN: 978 1 9152 6178 6

First published in 2026 by
Hachette Learning (a trading division of Hodder & Stoughton Limited),
An Hachette UK Company
Carmelite House
50 Victoria Embankment
London EC4Y 0DZ
www.HachetteLearning.com

The authorised representative in the EEA is Hachette Ireland, 8 Castlecourt Centre, Dublin 15, D15 XTP3, Ireland (email: info@hbgi.ie)

Impression number 10 9 8 7 6 5 4 3 2 1
Year 2030 2029 2028 2027 2026

Cover illustration by Oliver Caviglioli
Internal illustrations by DC Graphic Design Limited, Hextable, Kent.
Typeset in the UK.
Printed in the UK.

A catalogue record for this title is available from the British Library.

FSC www.fsc.org MIX Paper | Supporting responsible forestry FSC™ C104740

SERIES FOREWORD

This series of books was commissioned as a *Walkthrus* production to complement two other series: the *Teaching Walkthrus* Volumes 1, 2 and 3 and the *In Action* series. Together the *Walkthrus* team believe the books create a powerful resource for teachers and leaders in schools.

The *In Action* series is very popular with busy teachers. These short, easy-to-read guides tackle important ideas from education, cognitive science and research, and translate the research findings into key ideas and approaches teachers can explore, adopt and implement in their own practice.

Designed to link research with real-world classroom applications, the *In Action* series provides an accessible outline of key theories that teachers can apply to their practice in their own unique settings:

- *Annie Murphy Paul's The Extended Mind in Action*
- *Ausubel's Meaningful Learning in Action*
- *Bandura's Self-Efficacy Theory in Action*
- *Collins et al's Cognitive Apprenticeship in Action*
- *Nuthall's Hidden Lives of Learners in Action*
- *Bjork & Bjork's Desirable Difficulties in Action*
- *Dunlosky's Strengthening the Student Toolbox in Action*
- *Berger's An Ethic of Excellence in Action*
- *Wiliam & Leahy's Five Formative Assessment Strategies in Action*
- *Shimamura's MARGE Model of Learning in Action*
- *Sweller's Cognitive Load Theory in Action*
- *Fiorella & Mayer's Generative Learning in Action*
- *Rosenshine's Principles in Action*
- *Engelmann's Direct Instruction in Action*

The writers of each of the *In Action* books are all either serving teachers or teachers who taught for many years; this means the books' foci are grounded in the reality of teaching pupils in real classrooms.

Alongside the *In Action* series, the three-volume *Teaching Walkthrus* series is another resource designed to support busy teachers, with research-informed practical classroom strategies. Over 35,000 copies have now been distributed worldwide, supported by the online *Walkthrus* toolkit.

Each *Walkthrus* book is designed in six main series. Each *Walkthru* is a context-free, visual five-step guide of ideas, techniques and approaches to be explored and applied in individual classrooms. They are designed to be adaptable, accessible and easy to use within training, coaching and personal reflection. The five steps provide, not a rigid structure or set of rules, but a framework for thinking through an idea, deconstructed so that teachers can reconstruct it themselves in their own unique classrooms to enact powerful techniques.

With the *In Action* series providing a bridge between research and practice, and the *Walkthrus* providing a framework for exploring and refining pedagogy, the *Subjects In Action* series (such as *English in Action*) provides the third pillar: that of subject-specific support.

Each *In Action* subject book has been written by a primary subject expert who has sought to provide support, key information and ideas for subject leads and practising teachers in the primary phase. In primary, subject leads are often not subject specialists and colleagues are subject leads of more than one subject. This can be a real challenge for primary colleagues who are not immersed in a single subject discipline in the generalist primary classroom. These books are organised with a similar structure to their secondary counterparts so that primary teams can track key areas of focus across the whole series, making them easy to navigate and use as a connected suite of subject-lead resources.

It is no mean feat to capture the essence and spirit of a subject in a single volume and to balance the depth of detail of an entire subject community with a practical format to be used in multiple real-world classrooms.

These books are deliberately designed to be short in length but rich in support, practical advice and ideas, and all are written by highly experienced specialists who love their subjects and are passionate about practice in the primary phase.

This series is supportive enough for the non-specialist but rich enough to provide fresh avenues to explore for the experienced subject expert.

Editing the series has enabled me to see in sharp relief the unique beauty of each subject, brought skilfully to life by colleagues who truly love and champion their subject's place in the curriculum of our youngest children.

I hope you find this book and the wider series a professional friend – designed to help you develop your teaching and leading of each subject within the primary day. We have the opportunity in primary to accompany every pupil on their first steps into the formal academic disciplines; this book, I hope, is an invaluable companion when helping to plan the route.

Emma Turner

ABOUT THE AUTHOR

Kate's lifelong love of books began in childhood, where she spent endless hours immersed in story. Now, as both a teacher and a parent, one of her greatest joys and privileges is sharing her love of literature with children.

Born and raised in Canada, Kate began her teaching career with Regina Public Schools before moving to the UK in 2001. Since then, she has spent more than two decades working in Leeds schools, supporting children, teachers and school leaders. Throughout her career, she has held a variety of leadership roles, including English Lead, Leading Literacy Teacher for Leeds, Advanced Skills Teacher and Senior Leader with responsibility for Assessment.

Now, as a Primary English Consultant, Kate supports teachers in developing effective English practice and fostering a love of reading. She is also the creator of Scope for Imagination, where she reviews children's literature and collaborates with authors, illustrators and publishers to champion high-quality books for young readers. Passionate about connecting children with stories they will love, she is committed to helping teachers and families build rich reading experiences both in and beyond the classroom.

Kate is the author of the *Developing Reading Comprehension Skills* series, which provides practical, literature-rich resources designed to support reading development, strengthen comprehension and prepare pupils for assessment while nurturing a lifelong enjoyment of reading.

Kate lives in Leeds with her husband, three children and two much-loved cats.

ACKNOWLEDGEMENTS

This book is the culmination of years of learning, experiences and opportunities through the inspiration and encouragement of countless individuals in both Canada and the UK.

My sincere thanks to the Faculty of Education at the University of Regina and Coronation Park School for helping me discover the kind of teacher I wanted to become. Thank you to Drighlington Junior School and Farsley Farfield Primary School for challenging me to develop my practice, pursue my passions and grow as a leader. I am grateful to Abbey Grange Church of England Academy for the opportunity to explore secondary education through my role as a governor, broadening my understanding of teaching and learning beyond the primary phase.

Thank you to the children's book community on X and Instagram for welcoming me into a vibrant network of readers, educators, authors and publishers. My knowledge and appreciation of children's literature have grown immeasurably through our conversations. I am especially grateful to those who contributed a small part of their expertise to this book: Alex Barton, Jon Biddle, Dean Boddington, Nicki Cleveland, Sam Creighton, Erin Hamilton, Chris Harrison, Veronica Price and Richard Ruddick. My thanks also go to three inspiring teachers, Alex Galbraith, Micaela Romero and Stuart Tiffany, for generously sharing their best practice.

Special thanks to Emma Turner for her support in shaping the early drafts and for helping me navigate the challenge of distilling the vastness of primary English into a single book. I am enormously grateful to everyone at Hachette Learning for their expertise and guidance in bringing this book to life.

To my mum and dad, thank you for instilling in me a love of reading, an appreciation for education and the determination to always do my best. Dad, our weekly visits to the library mean more to me than you will ever know.

Finally, to my husband, Rob, and our three children, Charlie, Lucy and Tom: thank you for being my greatest supporters and biggest inspiration. Your love and encouragement have carried me through every challenge and new adventure.

REVIEWS

Kate has written the book I wish had existed when I first became an English Lead. It captures the complexity, joy and importance of teaching primary English without ever losing sight of how it actually works in the classroom. Every page offers practical ideas and suggestions, alongside a clear vision for what English can be when planned and taught effectively. I particularly liked how English is viewed in the context of the wider curriculum. It is a book that will help teachers nurture children who can communicate with confidence, and is ideal for teachers at all stages of their career.

Jon Biddle, Primary teacher and Reading for Pleasure advocate

An invaluable handbook on some of the very best ways we can teach reading, writing and oracy in the classroom of today. This is a treasure trove of inspiring pedagogy and practical, achievable activities – comprehensive and bang up-to-date, it's perfect for busy teachers.

Lucy Strange, Children's and YA author, former teacher and Reading for Pleasure advocate

Primary English in Action has reminded me just why I love English as a subject and why I think it's the most vital part of a child's education. I'm now scrabbling around to create a list of people I need to buy a copy for – whether that's to inspire them, guide them or to try to convince them that English is better than their subject.

Dean Boddington, Assistant Headteacher and Reading specialist

Primary English In Action is an essential CPD book for all English leads and SLT. Kate has skilfully explored the key areas of teaching English effectively through a research-based approach as well as practical strategies from those currently in schools. You will come away with so many ideas after reading this – it's inspiring!

Tom Griffiths, Headteacher and Children's book blogger, @checkemoutbooks

What a useful book this is! This is a great collection of simple, accessible actions and activities that school-based staff can easily digest and deploy. Written and presented in a straightforward, coherent way, Kate Heap has successfully collated a wealth of knowledge and experience that would help teachers at all stages of their careers – from trainees and ECTs to subject leaders and senior leaders. Primary English in Action is a great starting point for those looking to develop and refine their English offer in school.

Christopher Harrison, Headteacher at Oatlands Infant School

This resource is an absolute goldmine of information for any educator who is looking to strengthen their understanding and delivery of the primary English curriculum. Pedagogy is clearly and concisely explained, with a strong research base underpinning everything explored. There is also a treasure trove of strategies and techniques described to inspire readers to try something new with the young people they support.

Jo Cummins, Advisory primary school teacher and Reading consultant

Primary English in Action is a timely and valuable addition to every primary teacher's bookshelf. Kate brings together research, curriculum expertise and the realities of busy classrooms in a way that is both practical and inspiring. Her belief that speaking, reading and writing should be woven together, rather than taught as isolated strands, reflects the very best of primary practice.

What particularly stands out is the book's commitment to helping children develop not just the skills of literacy, but a genuine love of language, literature and communication. It is clear that every chapter has been written with teachers in mind, offering evidence-informed guidance alongside strategies that can be put into practice immediately.

Whether you are new to English leadership or an experienced practitioner, this is a book that will prompt reflection, strengthen practice and ultimately benefit the children in our classrooms.

Toria Bono, Year 4 leader and English champion

A compendium that is packed with practical approaches that underpin what we know about effective teaching of English.

Pie Corbett, Literacy expert, poet and author

Wow! Kate has fantastically captured the importance of the key aspects of the English Primary Curriculum along with actionable strategies for class teachers to put into practice. A must read for new and experienced teachers alike.

Andy Taylor, Senior lecturer at the University of Worcester and MrT of MrT's NQT and ECT support

Whether you are new to teaching primary English or an established leader or teacher, Kate's In Action book pulls together research, wisdom, experience and a huge amount of common sense. Teaching English in primary is fundamental to success for pupils across all other subjects; getting it right in English for our pupils means that teachers need to be informed, confident and inspired. Kate manages to make the potentially complex work of English teaching hugely accessible. This is an indispensable guide for anyone introducing our primary children to the joy and power of speaking, listening, writing and reading.

Emma Turner, FCCT

CONTENTS

Introduction: The big picture: English — xii

Chapter 1 Spoken language — 1

Chapter 2 Reading — 14

Chapter 3 Writing — 48

Chapter 4 Mode B: Non-instructional strategies — 76

Chapter 5 Debates and perspectives — 83

Chapter 6 Subject-specific research — 95

Chapter 7 Planning for primary English — 102

Chapter 8 Core reading spines — 125

Chapter 9 Misconceptions and difficult concepts — 131

Chapter 10 Assessment in primary English — 141

Chapter 11 Links with other subjects — 151

Chapter 12 Final reflections on primary English — 160

Acknowledgements — 162

References — 163

INTRODUCTION
THE BIG PICTURE: ENGLISH

If you plan, teach or support English in a primary school then this book is for you. You may be a subject lead, in your first term or your 20th year. Perhaps you teach a class of pupils across the primary age range and want to gather new ideas to take into reading, writing and spoken-language lessons. Maybe you're a teaching assistant working with pupils on a literacy programme, a trainee teacher or mentoring one. Most subject leads in primary schools aren't subject specialists. Many of us lead more than one subject – and usually do this as well as teaching a class full-time. I want this book to become your pocket companion: concise enough that you can pick it up during your busy week; comprehensive enough that it can help guide you through creating a vision for English across your whole school.

The book is split so you can read it from cover to cover or open it at the chapter you need. Each of the three curriculum strands – spoken language, reading and writing – has a chapter. These are split into two sections: 'Big Ideas', which lays out the research behind the practice, and 'In Action', which focuses on the classroom. There are also chapters that widen the scope to look at planning, assessment, some bigger debates in the profession and how English connects to the rest of the curriculum.

For me, primary English is so much more than just one subject. As it weaves through the curriculum and our daily lives, our understanding of English and literacy shapes who we are and who we become. There is great joy and privilege in guiding pupils as they discover their personal literacy: seeing a pupil find their reading spark and the right book that turns them into a reader; helping them develop their writer's voice that empowers them to share their thoughts with the world; or witnessing them gain the confidence to speak out and build relationships with others. These are milestones that reach far beyond the English lesson.

What is primary English all about?

The capabilities pupils develop in primary English are for life, not just their time in school. The backbone of everything we do, they allow us to connect with the rest of the world. The four elements of speaking, listening, reading and writing weave together to create individuals who are able to develop relationships, participate in the community, grow as people and feel able to make a difference.

As a primary school subject, English unlocks the rest of the curriculum for pupils. It allows them to explore history, analyse geography, investigate science and solve problems in maths. English provides pupils with the tools they need to understand language in a multitude of forms.

A literate pupil is far more likely to find success across the whole range of subject areas if they are effectively able to receive inward communication (listening and reading) and also express themselves through outward communication (speaking and writing) (Figure 0.1). This may be by listening to another person's point of view, reading for information, using writing skills to share what they know or discussing a new concept. Communicating fluently and confidently sets pupils on the road to becoming fully contributing members of society. The freedom that comes with being able to express themselves and understand the world is empowering. Through these four key areas of English, pupils acquire knowledge, develop their creativity and critical-thinking, find ways to express ideas and emotions, develop empathy and show the world who they are.

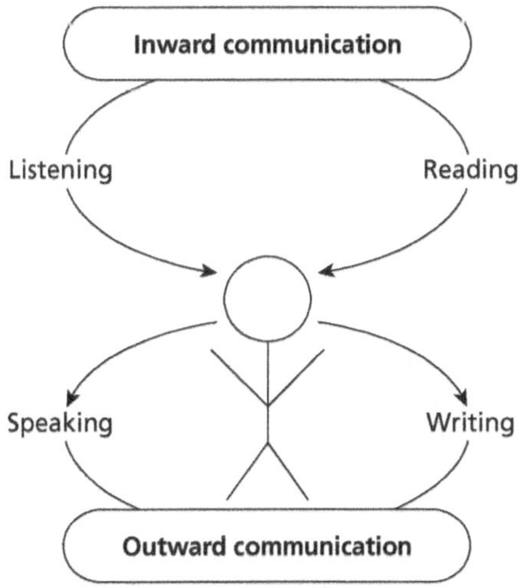

▲ Figure 0.1 The strands of English mapped onto inward communication (listening, reading) and outward communication (speaking, writing)

Children who learn to speak, listen, read and write effectively experience considerable advantages over those who do not. It is essential that schools address this need and provide the most impactful English provision possible to ensure pupils leave them with the skills necessary to continue to learn and grow. In an article in its 'Reading facts' briefing, the Reading Agency (2024) shares a list of statistics and relevant research related to the importance of reading. It reports that:

- one in four pupils hasn't reached the expected level of reading by the age of 11; many of these children will struggle to keep up at secondary school
- more recent PISA (Programme for International Student Assessment) data from 2022 show that 20% of 15-year-olds in the UK did not reach the minimum reading proficiency level, indicating that a substantial minority still leave compulsory schooling without secure reading skills (OECD, 2023)
- pupils are less able to learn other curricula if they do not develop sufficient reading skills by the middle of primary school.

Teachers can inspire pupils to continue to develop their speaking and listening, reading and writing throughout their lives by creating an environment where both pleasure and purpose are experienced and valued.

The strands of English in the national curriculum document are organised as three main areas: speaking, reading and writing. Alongside these is the spelling, phonics, vocabulary and grammar work that supports all three. They are the bones upon which everything else is built. I'll look at each in turn here and revisit them in detail in the following chapters.

Spoken language (oracy)

Oracy is the ability to communicate effectively using spoken language, encompassing both speaking and listening skills. It builds on previous national curriculum speaking and listening objectives (2006–2013), challenging pupils to think carefully about the language they use and tailor it to their subject, purpose and audience. Oracy comes into play across the primary curriculum, meaning it is not solely the responsibility of primary English despite many elements being rooted in English aims and objectives. Developing oracy skills inspires critical and creative thought, clear expression and appreciation for the points of view of others, while building vocabulary. Pupils gain an understanding of the structures of language, which support both reading and writing. If children are able to say it, they are much more likely to be able to write it.

The Oracy All-Party Parliamentary Group (APPG, 2021) reported that oracy has a notable impact on:

- academic outcomes
- language development, vocabulary acquisition and literacy
- quality of teaching
- wellbeing, mental health and social and emotional skills
- confidence and self-esteem
- progression to further or higher education
- employability
- citizenship and agency.

Primary teachers develop oracy through fostering high-quality classroom talk, modelling language structures and expression and by providing opportunities for intentionally planned speaking and listening activities.

I explore this in depth in Chapter 1, in the section titled 'Spoken language: the Big Ideas'.

Reading

Reading a wide range of literature provides children with a window to the world both now and in the past, as well as providing a vision for the future. Readers are given opportunities to develop culturally, emotionally, intellectually, socially and spiritually. Teachers and librarians have the potential to harness the power of words to build a more empathetic generation where pupils are presented with alternative points of view. Through rich, diverse and varied stories, children may experience situations they have not encountered in their own lives. They begin to understand how others might feel and how they can help. Books are key for developing thoughtful, caring individuals who want to support the people around them.

This breadth of reading opportunity also allows children to experience the richness of British culture. One of the greatest strengths of contemporary literature is the diversity of stories, characters and authors. Children are able to see elements of their own lives mirrored in books more now than ever before. Representation of a range of ethnicities, cultures, religions, socioeconomic levels, families, abilities, genders and sexual orientation is increasing. There is still a long way to go, but many publishers are striving to improve the choice readers find on bookshelves. When a child is able to identify with a character in a book, they feel empowered and valued. They see that their life, their story, matters.

One way to think about the power of stories is through author Rudine Sims Bishop's metaphor describing books as windows, mirrors and sliding glass doors. She writes that books are windows that allow children to see into other worlds, both real and fictional; they can serve as sliding glass doors (Sims Bishop, 1990) that children walk right through to enter and inhabit the worlds within books; and, when crafted in just the right way, 'a book can also be a mirror'. Books become literal mirrors when they reflect children's lives and help them recognise their experiences within the larger context of humanity. Through reading, Bishop argues, children learn about others and learn about themselves. Both are important. Reading Sims Bishop's essay is a reminder that texts are powerful. When we decide which books to put in front of pupils (and which to leave out), we are making decisions about what they learn about who people are and who they can be.

Immersion in quality literature supports the development of a wide vocabulary. Pupils are able to explore and appreciate the richness of language, learning words they may not otherwise encounter. Exploring classic and contemporary poetry allows children to play with language. As they experiment with sound, rhythm and word choice, they discover layers of meaning rich with symbolism and nuance. Quality non-fiction provides children with more technical vocabulary, pushing them to read, speak and write at a higher level and understand the information texts that fill our world.

Primary English provides pupils with the building blocks for a lifetime of reading. Whether it's exploring the rhythm and language of a nursery rhyme, the lyrical patterns of a poem, the excitement of an adventure story or the fascinating facts of a non-fiction book, teachers take pupils on a reading journey. Through powerful modelling, provision of high-quality books and opportunities for positive reading experiences, both individually and as a group, teachers set the tone and expectation that reading is something we all do, not because we have to but because we truly enjoy it and it enriches our lives. Reading for pleasure helps to ensure children leave primary school with the drive to continue learning and growing through books.

I explore this in depth in Chapter 2, in the section titled 'Reading: the Big Ideas'.

Writing

From letter formation and phonics to early spelling and creating stories and non-fiction texts, finding a purpose for writing is essential. Knowing why they're writing and who will read it motivates pupils to write more often and inspires them to do the best they can.

During their time in primary school, pupils learn to write for a range of purposes. Whether it's to entertain, inform, reflect, explain or persuade, they must be given the tools to express themselves coherently and fluently.

Writing is incredibly challenging. It is so much more than having neat handwriting or composing a grammatically correct sentence. Children must learn to combine multiple elements at word, sentence and text level with imagination and / or information to create something that is not only readable but engaging as well.

Like reading for pleasure, writing for pleasure is key to developing expressive, imaginative writers for life. Children who enjoy putting pen to paper (or writing on a computer) will be much more likely to continue expressing themselves in this way into adulthood and achieve more academically. The research report 'What is it Writing for Pleasure teachers do that makes the difference?' (Young, 2019) shows that a Writing for Pleasure pedagogy greatly impacts a writer's affective domains (involving feelings, attitudes and emotions) and sense of achievement.

Ross Young captures what is at stake when writing becomes meaningful for a child: 'Writing for pleasure therefore gives children a feeling of empowerment and that their writing has enriched their life and the lives of others' (Young, 2021).

It is a high aim, and a realistic one when the conditions are right. Young describes six affective domains that together make up a writer's identity:

1. Identity as a writer: I am
2. Volition to write: I want to
3. Motivation to write: I know why
4. Sense of self-efficacy: I can do this
5. Agency: I have a say
6. Self-regulation: I know what to do and how to do it.

This matters because the numbers are currently running in the wrong direction. Research from the National Literacy Trust (2023) showed a decline in the number of children who find pleasure in writing. Key findings in 2023 revealed that only 34.6% of children and young people aged 8 to 18 said they enjoy writing in their free time. Only 19.3% of children said they wrote something daily in their free time, whereas in 2010, 28.5% said they wrote daily. Unfortunately, this trend continued to decline in 2024, with fewer than 3 in 10 children (28.7%) saying they enjoyed writing in their free time. Enjoyment levels also dropped in 2024, particularly among boys aged 5 to 8 (National Literacy Trust, 2024).

It is so important that schools strive to increase pupils' positive experiences around writing, while providing them with meaningful reasons to write regularly. Schools should aim for pupils to write with enjoyment as well as with satisfaction. In Ross Young's 'A writing for pleasure manifesto' (2021), writing for pleasure is described as having two aspects: writing *as* pleasure (enjoyment) and writing *with* pleasure (satisfaction). When children experience writing *as* pleasure, they feel compelled to write and find fun or enjoyment in doing it. They are confident and happy when engaging with the different processes of writing and feel part of a writing community in which they can share their writing and support other writers. When writing *with* pleasure, the satisfaction comes in the sense of achievement and pride having completed the piece of writing. Children are finding their voice as writers and are happy to share their ideas with others.

Both aspects of writing for pleasure are important as children begin to identify as writers, developing agency, a unique voice and desire to write. Teachers can create an environment that fosters both enjoyment and satisfaction in writing.

As you'll see in Chapter 3, in the section titled 'Writing: the Big Ideas', writing, spelling, grammar, vocabulary and phonics are integrated into that chapter and into a subsequent section, titled 'Spelling: instructional strategies'. They are not broken out into their own separate curriculum area. This was a conscious decision. I feel that they are most effectively taught as part of learning to read and write, not in isolation as separate skills.

The aims of primary English

The aims of primary English are set out by the national curriculum. In every school, teachers and leaders should aim to promote high standards of language and literacy by equipping pupils with a strong command of the spoken and written word, and to develop their love of literature through widespread reading for enjoyment (DfE, 2013b).

This is broken down into seven smaller aims that provide structure for English provision.

> The national curriculum for English aims to ensure that all pupils:
>
> - read easily, fluently and with good understanding
> - develop the habit of reading widely and often, for both pleasure and information
> - acquire a wide vocabulary, an understanding of grammar and knowledge of linguistic conventions for reading, writing and spoken language
> - appreciate our rich and varied literary heritage
> - write clearly, accurately and coherently, adapting their language and style in and for a range of contexts, purposes and audiences
> - use discussion in order to learn; they should be able to elaborate and explain clearly their understanding and ideas
> - are competent in the arts of speaking and listening, making formal presentations, demonstrating to others and participating in debate.
>
> **DfE (2013b, p.3)**

How this book is organised

Primary English is sometimes spoken and written about as though its strands – spoken language, reading, writing, spelling and grammar – were bits of curriculum to be taught discretely. My argument in this book is that they aren't discrete at all. They're a single set of powerfully intertwined capabilities, and children learn them best when we teach them together.

Chapters 1, 2 and **3** unpack each of the three national curriculum strands – spoken language, reading and writing – in turn, and the connections between them will become clear as you read. Each 'Big Ideas' section sets out the research / craft knowledge and the curriculum expectations; each 'In Action' section turns to classroom practice.

Chapter 4 explores Mode B: the things that teachers do around their lessons that build reading and writing culture in their schools. **Chapter 5** tackles three hot-topic debates in primary English at the moment – whole-class versus group guided reading; how schools handle home reading; and traditional spelling tests – and I give you my own opinion on each. **Chapter 6** is a handy reference list of the subject-specific researchers, organisations and resources I keep going back to.

From **Chapter 7**, the focus shifts to planning and leadership in the subject. **Chapter 7** works through progression maps, curriculum maps, topic sequences and lesson plans at macro, medium and micro timescales. **Chapter 8** looks at core reading spines: how to select and curate texts to form the backbone of your school's reading curriculum. **Chapter 9** addresses those tricky concepts and misconceptions children and adults get stuck on. **Chapter 10** is about assessment and the eternal debate about attainment versus progress. **Chapter 11** looks outwards to English's links with the rest of the primary curriculum. **Chapter 12** is my final word.

My hope is that you'll finish this book seeing English as the connective tissue that holds the primary curriculum together and that you'll feel equipped to build an English provision in your school that sends children out as readers, writers and speakers for life.

Further reading

Oracy All-Party Parliamentary Group (2021) 'Speak for Change', www.education-uk.org/documents/pdfs/2021-appg-oracy.pdf

The Reading Agency (2024) 'Reading facts', https://readingagency.org.uk/our-work/our-research/reading-facts/

Young, R. (2019) 'What is it Writing for Pleasure teachers do that makes the difference?', https://writing4pleasure.com/what-is-it-writing-for-pleasure-teachers-do-that-makes-the-difference-research-report/

CHAPTER 1
SPOKEN LANGUAGE

Spoken language: the Big Ideas

Of the four strands of primary English, speaking and listening are arguably those I see change most rapidly in a classroom environment. We all know the pupil who finds it difficult to record a sentence accurately on paper. Yet these are often the same pupils who will talk their idea through with a partner and astound you with their ability to communicate accurately what they actually know. For this reason, the national curriculum rightly places such emphasis on spoken language. Not only does it ask teachers to make sure pupils can 'use discussion in order to learn', but it also expects teachers to help pupils become 'competent in the arts of speaking and listening, making formal presentations, demonstrating to others and participating in debate'. This isn't an add-on. Far from it. These skills form the bedrock on which all other aspects of English are built.

I'll never forget the 10-year-old First Nations boy I taught in Canada. He spent considerable time on a reserve with his grandparents, missing a lot of school in the city. As a result, he struggled with English and maths. During our study of Canadian First Nations culture, we visited the Museum of Natural History. When the guide asked a question, this boy was able to answer in incredible detail, then continued sharing everything he knew about his culture. The guide stepped back, allowing him to lead the rest of the tour. Even though he might struggle to read an information book or write about his knowledge, this child was engaged, inspired and empowered to talk about his area of expertise.

As I explained in the Introduction, there are four intricately connected strands to primary English: speaking, listening, reading and writing. This chapter deals with just speaking and listening. It explains what high-quality oracy provision entails, considers why the current focus on spoken language is so important and details how you can implement those principles in your classroom practice. Many of the ideas covered in this chapter carry through into the rest of the book: the readers who preview a text through discussion in Chapter 2 and the writers who 'talk aloud' to plan their ideas in Chapter 3 are utilising the oracy skills highlighted in this chapter.

Oracy is the ability to articulate ideas, develop understanding and engage with others through spoken language (Voice 21, 'What is oracy?'). Oracy education, along with dialogic teaching (learning through talk in dialogue with teachers), is key to children's development – cognitively, socially and linguistically. These skills lay the foundation for all other areas of learning and can be found across the curriculum (Cambridge Assessment International Education, 2022).

It is essential that the language of the classroom is rich and varied. As adults model vocabulary and language structures, children hear, process and then imitate as they experiment with new ways of speaking. The more pupils have opportunities to speak in school, the more effective they become.

It is essential that oracy development in key stage 1 grows out of the focus on communication and language in the Early Years Foundation Stage Framework (DfE, 2024) – which itself underpins all other areas of learning across the Early Years Foundation Stage (EYFS). Pupils who have not yet reached a good level of development (GLD) in EYFS should continue to be supported in those objectives.

Voice 21 is the UK's oracy education charity. It works with schools to transform the learning and life chances of young people through talk, campaigning for oracy to have a higher status in the education system. In addition to its campaign, Voice 21 has created resources sharing its research and helping schools develop a plan for oracy (available on its website, voice21.org). The most instantly useful of these tools is Voice 21's Oracy Framework (which we cover later in this chapter), which demystifies a broad concept into four discrete strands, and includes lesson plans, assessment guidance and training to embed it school-wide.

Oracy is receiving well-deserved attention in current education and government contexts. Having been somewhat overlooked in recent years, projects such as Voice 21 are giving it the focus it deserves. An increasing number of schools are creating oracy objectives as a part of their school development plans, and developing projects that will enable their pupils to experience greater success through their ability to express themselves orally. This is far from a new idea. Almost six decades ago, James Britton wrote 'Reading and writing float on a sea of talk' (Britton, 1970). That principle continues to shape classroom strategies today, using talk to help pupils comprehend what they read and develop what they write.

Writing in Will Millard and Loic Menzies' report on spoken language in English schools, Beccy Earnshaw (former CEO of Voice 21) and Peter Hyman (former executive headteacher of School 21 – the East London secondary where Voice 21 developed the original oracy approach) set out why oracy is so important in schools:

> The things we say and how we say them can inform, influence, inspire and motivate others and express our empathy, understanding and creativity. It is our ability to communicate that enables us to build positive relationships, collaborate for common purpose, deliberate and share our ideas as citizens.
>
> **Millard and Menzies (2016)**

I keep coming back to those last words... 'as citizens'. We teach oracy for more than school success: we teach pupils how to speak for life beyond school, to have their voices heard, to listen well and to argue without fighting. Through rich experiences such as guiding Year 4 through preparation for a debate or listening to a Reception pupil teach their friend something on the carpet, adult skills are developed one conversation at a time. That is why speech is placed before reading and writing.

Levels of formality

Exploring levels of formality teaches pupils that in different situations, people speak in different ways. Conversations on the playground may differ from classroom discussions or how pupils speak to the headteacher. Vocabulary choices, sentence structure and gestures tend to match the level of formality required. Teachers can encourage pupils to explore the difference between informal and formal speech by role-playing conversations and thinking about how we speak to people in our lives.

Temple Learning Academy has produced a useful short video modelling a primary Formality Scale in action (see 'Further reading').

Three tiers of vocabulary

Introduced by Dr Isabel Beck and Dr Margaret McKeown of the University of Pittsburgh in *Bringing Words to Life: Robust Vocabulary Instruction* (2002), tiered vocabulary is a method for categorising words into three tiers according to their frequency, complexity and meaning. Each tier requires a different approach.

Tier one

Tier one words are a key part of everyday language. These high-frequency words do not need to be taught explicitly because they are picked up through talk with family members, peers and teachers. Examples of tier one words include *cat*, *shoe* and *snow*.

Tier two

Tier two words are more academic in nature: cross-curricular vocabulary that appears throughout the school day. As tier two words do not always come up in everyday conversation, they require direct instruction. Spending time exploring tier two vocabulary will have a great impact on reading and writing skills in all subject areas. Examples of tier two words include *complete*, *possible* and *recognise*.

Tier three

Tier three words occur only in specific areas of learning. Because they are often central to understanding in their academic subject area, they should be built into lessons. Pre-teaching tier three vocabulary can have a positive impact on pupils who need extra support or for whom English is an additional language. Examples of tier three words include *atom* in science, *peninsula* in geography and *denominator* in maths.

If you visit the Vocabulary Ninja website, you'll find lists of year-by-year tier two words for pupils from Reception through to Year 6 (see 'Further reading'). Rather than trying to think of words yourself every time you start a new topic, these lists provide suggestions, so you can build them into the week's reading, writing and talk. Flicking through the list will often remind you of words you assumed the class knew already, or words you have been accidentally teaching as tier three when they're actually cross-curricular tier two.

Further oracy skills to practise in the classroom

In addition to these foundational speaking and listening skills, pupils are acquiring a constellation of others – and these fall, conveniently, into four categories.

Some are *physical* skills: how children use their voices (loudness, tone, clarity) and their bodies (eye contact, gesture, posture). Some are *linguistic*: reaching for a more specific vocabulary – vocabulary that might be ambitious, technical or related to a specific subject – and matching the formality of their language to their audience and situation (are they in the playground, in the classroom, at assembly, talking to a visitor from another school?). Others are *cognitive*: building on each other's ideas, explaining their thinking and asking authentic questions, rather than simply waiting for their chance to speak so they can repeat what they were planning to say. Finally, there are *social and emotional skills*: appearing to listen to others, sharing the conversation and making space for those more timid voices to be heard.

Spoken language is key to pupils' development of reading and writing across the whole primary curriculum. As they listen to language being used by parents and carers, teachers and classmates, they absorb vocabulary and grammatical constructions. The quality and range of these language models have a powerful effect on how well they understand and communicate.

Spoken language in reading

Pupils should be encouraged to explain their understanding of what they have read – sharing thoughts about the illustrations, key plot points, inferences and predictions. Asking questions, exploring the author's use of language, making comparisons and summarising ideas allows pupils to make their thinking clear to themselves as well as to others. Discussion is a shared experience that prompts children to listen to others, imitate their responses and develop their own clear communication skills.

Spoken language in writing

By talking about what they have read and vocalising ideas before writing, pupils have the opportunity to rehearse what they want to write, making sure it makes sense and is what they actually want to say. Teachers are able to explore misconceptions and give pupils the tools to talk through their learning.

The skills of discussion, debate and drama give pupils even more opportunities to express themselves, push the limits of their abilities and grow as confident and effective communicators.

Links across the curriculum

A focus on spoken language, or oracy, across the curriculum will accelerate progress in English, as pupils grasp a deeper understanding of language and how it is used for specific purposes.

Every voice counts

A 2021 inquiry by the Oracy All-Party Parliamentary Group (APPG) found that oracy impacts:

- academic outcomes
- language development, vocabulary acquisition and literacy
- quality of teaching
- wellbeing, mental health and social and emotional skills
- confidence and self-esteem
- progression to further or higher education
- employability
- citizenship and agency.

Schools involved in the APPG Voice 21 initiative not only report increased progress and attainment but also positive developments in pupils' confidence in their ability to articulate their ideas and share in class.

National curriculum expectations for spoken language in primary

The national curriculum (DfE, 2013c) provides 12 statutory requirements for spoken language at key stages 1 and 2. Guidance outlines that schools should teach the content for these statements at a level appropriate to the age of the pupils and build on the oral language skills they have previously been taught.

These objectives are not tied to English lessons and should be developed across the curriculum.

The 12 requirements are that pupils should be taught to:

1. listen and respond appropriately to adults and their peers
2. ask relevant questions to extend their understanding and knowledge
3. use relevant strategies to build their vocabulary
4. articulate and justify answers, arguments and opinions
5. give well-structured descriptions, explanations and narratives for different purposes, including for expressing feelings
6. maintain attention and participate actively in collaborative conversations, staying on topic and initiating and responding to comments

7 use spoken language to develop understanding through speculating, hypothesising, imagining and exploring ideas
8 speak audibly and fluently, with an increasing command of Standard English
9 participate in discussions, presentations, performances, role play, improvisations and debates
10 gain, maintain and monitor the interest of the listener(s)
11 consider and evaluate different viewpoints, attending to and building on the contributions of others
12 select and use appropriate registers for effective communication.

Spoken language in action: instructional strategies

Teaching strategies are always evolving, often coming back around to high-quality practice seen before. The current focus on oracy draws on many of the ideas from speaking and listening programmes of previous English frameworks, enhancing them and providing opportunities to take pupils' skills even further.

The Oracy Framework from Voice 21 and Oracy Cambridge (2020) focuses on four key skills:

1. **Physical** – the use of voice (pace, tone, pronunciation and projection) and body language (gestures, postures, facial expression and eye contact)
2. **Linguistic** – appropriate vocabulary choice, language choices (register and grammar) and rhetorical techniques
3. **Cognitive** – content (own content and building on the views of others), structure, clarifying and summarising, self-regulation (focus and time management) and reasoning (giving reasons to support views and critically examining views)
4. **Social and emotional** – working with others, listening and responding, confidence and audience awareness.

Helping pupils to understand and develop their skills in each of these four areas will enable them to become articulate and confident speaking in a variety of situations.

The Oracy Framework and the 'It's good to talk: oracy lesson plan' produced by Voice 21 (British Council, The Commonwealth and Voice 21,

2021) provide teachers with clear guidance on how to introduce these skills and encourage children to think about their own oracy development.

Oracy can be developed across a range of lessons and subject areas by:

- teaching talk skills for group work and collaborative learning
- teaching presentational skills
- teaching debating skills
- teaching listening skills.

Cambridge Assessment International Education (2022)

The Primary National Strategy of 2003 to 2011 promoted speaking and listening in primary schools. The posters from 'Speaking, listening and learning: working with children in key stages 1 and 2' (DfES, 2024) provided a wealth of key teaching points and practical ideas – many of which are worth revisiting. They may be used in English lessons and other subjects to give pupils as many opportunities as possible to develop their communication skills. Here follows a small sample of the activities included.

Speaking

Voice over

Whether it's putting on a puppet show or creating a video with voice over, planning, rehearsing and performing a short story will help pupils develop and refine their script while reflecting on volume, intonation and expression. The real magic, I've found, is in the playback; there is nothing like hearing their own recorded voice to make a Year 3 reader suddenly very interested in pace and tone.

Radio broadcast

Begin by listening to good examples of radio shows together. Ask pupils to observe what the hosts do: no gestures, no eye contact, no contact with their audience at all – voice only. After experiencing it done well, choose topics that involve explaining and reasoning or trying to persuade the listener.

Debates

Debates offer a fantastic opportunity to explore persuasive language, formality and speaking with authority.

- Take some time to review effective persuasive language before beginning the activity.
- Choose an argument with two clear sides.
- Split the class into two groups to debate each side of the argument.
- Give groups time to prepare: collect ideas to support their point of view, organise main points, plan opening and closing statements, predict what the other side might say and write counter arguments.
- The teacher chairs the debate.
- At the end, give everyone an anonymous vote on which side they agree with most. Discuss whether the debate has caused them to change their mind. Who was a powerful speaker? Why?

Listening

Barrier games

This strategy focuses on giving and receiving instructions. Pupils must choose their words carefully and really listen to what their partner is saying.

- Pupils sit back to back or on either side of a screen.
- The speaker describes something in detail: an object, a picture they've drawn, a model they've built, directions on a map.
- The listener tries to recreate the thing being described without looking. They may ask questions to clarify as the interaction goes on.
- When finished, ask the pupils to turn around, or remove the screen, to compare their results.

Draw a story

This is a lovely quiet-time activity that also works really well.

- Choose a story or section of a story with clear plot points.
- Read aloud while pupils listen.
- Pause at logical stopping points and ask pupils to draw something to represent that part of the story.
- At the end of the story ask pupils to reflect on what it was about and work in pairs to retell the story from their drawings.

Guided listening

Listening frames can help pupils focus when listening to a presentation, guest speaker or video.

- Ask pupils to write questions before listening, then to try to find the answers to these questions while they listen.
- Give pupils headings to help them listen for specific information.
- Encourage pupils to create a picture in their heads as they listen or to draw small sketches of key information.

Group discussion

Think-pair-share

Go beyond partner talk by encouraging pupils to listen carefully to more points of view, take on board new ideas and come to a consensus.

- Ask pupils to consider a problem or issue individually.
- Move into pairs. Ask pupils to explain their ideas to their partner, discuss the issue and come to a joint conclusion.
- Each pair may feed back to the class, or two pairs may join to make a four. Each pair shares their ideas and the larger group forms a conclusion together.
- Teachers may wish to stop at this point and feed back to the whole class, or continue to snowball the discussion into groups of eight, sixteen and, finally, the whole class.

Jigsaw

The jigsaw group strategy is perfect for efficiently investigating and sharing new information. For example, the task might be to produce an information booklet about foxes: appearance, habitat, behaviour and diet. Rather than each pupil researching every aspect, groups work together and share information.

- Organise the class into home groups.
- Number each pupil in a home group 1, 2, 3 or 4. Give each number a topic to research and discuss (e.g. 1 = appearance, 2 = habitat, 3 = behaviour, 4 = diet).
- Move into expert groups (all the 1s together, all the 2s together, and so on).

- Expert groups research their topic, discuss their findings and make notes.
- The pupils move back into their home groups and each takes it in turn to feed back what they found out in their expert group.
- This is also a useful strategy for discussing and giving feedback on questions about a text or a particular issue.

Statements game

A group is given a set of cards with a statement written on each. Through discussion, the group agrees on how to categorise the statements (this could be true / false, agree / disagree or ranked in order of importance.

Drama

Conscience alley

Conscience alley gives pupils an opportunity to explore a character's mind at a key moment of dilemma or decision-making.

- Pupils stand in two lines facing each other.
- One pupil takes on the role of the character. As they walk down the alley between the two lines, each pupil voices a thought for the character, speaking as their conscience.
- You may wish for one line to voice positive thoughts while the other voices negative thoughts.
- When the pupil in role reaches the end of the lines, they consider all that has been said and make a decision.

Thought tracking

Thought tracking gives pupils opportunities to consider the thoughts of characters.

- Start pupils off in a freeze frame, or in a role play where you can freeze the action.
- Ask the rest of the class to contribute ideas as if they were saying the thoughts of one of the characters aloud.
- The class might form a circle around a character and each say a thought, or individual pupils might stand next to the frozen character and speak their thoughts aloud.

Meetings

Role-playing a town-hall-style meeting gives pupils an opportunity to take on a specific role within a larger group.

- Introduce a scenario in which a meeting is necessary so a group can come to a collective decision (e.g. 'The council wants to build a wind farm near the coast. Where should it be located?').
- Organise the pupils into different groups, each with an interest in the decision to be made (e.g. farmers, home owners, property developers, nature conservationists).
- In role, the teacher leads the meeting, giving each group an opportunity to share their point of view, question others and come to a decision.

Whole-school initiatives

No Pens Day

No Pens Day is an initiative introduced by Speech and Language UK, with the aim of raising awareness of the importance of talking and understanding of words. Schools from early years settings right through to colleges are encouraged to plan a day of fun and engaging activities that focus on spoken language rather than paper and pencil tasks. This is a great way to encourage all teachers to widen their repertoire of spoken language activities. It is also very helpful for teachers; planning a day where you don't use writing illuminates how often we tell pupils to 'write it down' when explaining something, when a conversation would achieve exactly the same result, if not better.

Speech and Language UK has lots of lesson plans and resources on its website for schools that take part (see 'Further reading'). One of the easiest ways to get started is to take a lesson you already teach confidently, remove all the written elements and then work out how you could achieve the same learning outcomes using spoken language only. Discussion, drama, explaining your thinking to a partner... you'll soon see that your lesson isn't compromised by cutting out the writing.

Talk for Writing

Talk for Writing is an approach to teaching English in primary and secondary schools. Developed by Pie Corbett and supported by Julia Strong, it focuses on helping pupils internalise the language structures needed to write, through 'talking the text' and close reading. At the beginning of each unit, pupils spend time getting to know a model text very well through reading, listening, speaking, dramatising, investigating and playing with language. This oral involvement allows them to internalise and personalise the text in preparation for their own writing later. For website details, see 'Further reading'.

Further reading

British Council, The Commonwealth and Voice 21 (2021) 'It's good to talk: oracy lesson plan', www.britishcouncil.org/sites/default/files/its_good_to_talk.pdf

Cambridge Assessment International Education (2022) 'Education brief: oracy'. Cambridge University Press and Assessment, www.cambridgeinternational.org/Images/661428-education-brief-oracy-.pdf

Department for Education and Skills (2004) 'Speaking, listening and learning: working with children in key stages 1 and 2'. DfES 0163-2004

Oracy All-Party Parliamentary Group (2021) 'Speak for change', www.education-uk.org/documents/pdfs/2021-appg-oracy.pdf

Speech and Language UK, lesson plans and other resources for schools that take part in No Pens Day, https://speechandlanguage.org.uk/get-involved/no-pens-day/

Talk for Writing focuses on helping children internalise the language structures needed to write, through 'talking the text' and close reading, www.talk4writing.com

Temple Learning Academy, 'The Formality Scale – Primary' [video], www.youtube.com/watch?v=LfhVVDTKdHk

Vocabulary Ninja, list of tier two vocabulary for Reception to Year 6, available to download from https://vocabularyninja.co.uk/shop/tier-2-words/

Voice 21 and Oracy Cambridge (2020) 'The Oracy Framework', https://membership-hub.voice21.org/the-oracy-framework

CHAPTER 2
READING

Reading: the Big Ideas

As educators, there are so many things we teach pupils in primary school that they return to throughout their lives. However, there's one skill I find myself thinking about daily that has such a profound impact – reading. Not only is it the doorway into every other subject on the curriculum but it is also one of the most valuable tools we have to help mould our pupils into who they will become. I have watched pupils find their voice when reading aloud; witnessed a reluctant reader devour book after book after discovering just the right one; and felt an entire classroom collectively hold their breath at a key moment in a shared novel. Creating a classroom environment where reading is loved and fully explored is one of the most important things we can do to ensure our pupils become happy, caring and engaged members of society.

Reading has a huge impact on pupils' learning across the curriculum. It improves their understanding of the world, builds vocabulary, improves spelling, develops speaking and listening, influences their writing and broadens their general knowledge. Time spent reading has a powerful impact on children's futures and their relationships with others. Reading builds empathy and gives us all a greater understanding of diverse situations we may not otherwise experience. At the heart of every primary school, there must be an intentional, teacher-led drive to build a community of readers.

This chapter sits at the centre of the three curriculum strands explored in this book. The spoken language strategies introduced in Chapter 1 underpin the rich discussion that brings reading to life; in turn, the reading culture we build here feeds directly into the writing pedagogy explored in Chapter 3: children who read widely and well become writers with something to say. Reading is not a stand-alone subject. It is the thread that runs through every element of primary English and, indeed, every subject in the primary classroom.

The national curriculum sets out that the programmes of study for reading at key stages 1 and 2 consist of two dimensions: word reading and comprehension. These two dimensions go hand in hand to create confident, fluent, thoughtful readers, and effective teaching attends to both.

Word reading involves decoding (applying knowledge of letter–sound relationships, including knowledge of letter patterns, to pronounce written words correctly) and recognition of familiar words. The teaching of phonics is a key part of early years provision and key stage 1.

Good comprehension develops from a strong vocabulary, an understanding of grammar and knowledge of the world. As children read a wide variety of quality fiction, non-fiction and poetry, they should be encouraged to make links with their own lives and experiences. Guided discussion with adults and peers will solidify this comprehension and challenge children to think more deeply about what they have read.

Year 1 teachers should be mindful of pupils' progress towards the areas of learning in the Early Years Foundation Stage (EYFS) Framework. Just because they have started Year 1 does not mean they are ready to access the national curriculum. Teachers should be aiming to help pupils reach that EYFS good level of development (GLD) in literacy. Spending time on songs, rhymes and early decoding skills is essential for building a lifelong love of reading.

Building blocks of reading

Reading is a complex task in which pupils draw upon a variety of strategies and skills to make sense of a text. None can occur in isolation.

Phonics

Phonics helps children learn to read by teaching them to hear, identify and use the sounds found in words. Children learn the phonemes (sounds) associated with graphemes (letters), first pronouncing them in isolation then blending them together to read words.

When teaching Phonics, it is essential that teachers follow the school's policy and use the agreed Phonics scheme. Year 1 and 2 teachers work closely with teachers in EYFS to develop a plan for teaching and assessment.

Fluency

Often described as the bridge between decoding and comprehension, fluency occurs when children are able to decode words accurately without having to stop and think about them (Green, 2021). This automatic reading allows them to move through a text efficiently, focusing on meaning and comprehension.

Vocabulary

Understanding word meaning is key across all areas of English. The more children speak with others, read widely and encounter a variety of life experiences, the stronger their vocabulary will become. When reading, pupils first make use of the vocabulary they already know. When they come across an unfamiliar word, they need to use strategies for working out meaning from context or knowledge of similar words.

Sense of story and sequence

From a young age, children learn to retell a story and develop the concept of plot. Signpost words such as 'first', 'then' and 'next' help them spot key elements and predict what might happen next.

Retrieval

Retrieval is the ability to pick out key pieces of information from the text. This might be the name of a character, a plot point or a fact about the topic. It is a basic tool of comprehension, allowing a child to demonstrate they've understood the main details of what they've read.

Activating and using background knowledge

When reading, children who make links to their background knowledge are better able to make inferences and interpret the meaning of unknown words. After reading, any new knowledge gained becomes part of their background knowledge, building greater foundations for future success. It is sometimes the case that life experience and wider knowledge can outweigh reading ability when it comes to comprehension. That is why it is so important for teachers to provide real-life experiences and opportunities to develop knowledge before reading.

Generating and asking questions

Learning to ask questions while reading activates pupils' critical-thinking while improving memory and overall comprehension. Teachers can support pupils in the depth of their questioning by teaching them about Bloom's Taxonomy of Questions and providing prompts to help them shape their questions. Include question prompts linked to remembering, understanding, applying, analysing, evaluating and creating (Sedita, 2023).

Inference and prediction

Using inference to work out what's going on around us is key. When reading, inference allows children to dig deeper into the text, beyond basic decoding and retrieval, and really make sense of the author's meaning. Because authors don't provide us with every detail, using inference encourages children to activate their background knowledge and look for clues in the text to help extend their understanding.

Visualising

Visualising is a strategy in which readers form pictures in their minds as they read. It deepens understanding and improves memory of what has been read. This is also an effective way for children to monitor their comprehension. Like most reading strategies, it must be taught by drawing children's attention to it, modelling and practice (PRIDE Reading Program, 2023).

Understanding the author's use of language

Much of the beauty in reading comes through an author's use of descriptive word choice and figurative language. As children develop an understanding of devices such as simile, metaphor, personification and alliteration, they are able to appreciate the author's purpose and the deeper meaning of the text.

Summary

Summarising involves identifying the key points in a text and pulling them together to establish the main idea. This may include understanding subheadings, pulling out themes and discussing the gist of what has been read.

Comparison

When making comparisons, children identify how characters, settings and events in a text are similar to or different from each other. They may also identify how a character changes over the course of a story.

Monitoring comprehension

As children read, it's important they check everything makes sense. When it doesn't, they should pause and use a variety of strategies to help. They might reread the sentence, think about what the author is trying to say, work out the meaning of an unknown word using the context of the sentence or paragraph, think about similar words they already know or ask an adult or classmate for help. They may also ask themselves questions as they read, summarise what they've read or make predictions about what might come next. Some readers will do this intuitively, while others will need to be taught to consider their comprehension and take steps to repair it when it goes wrong (Iris Reading, 2022).

Text types and author's purpose

Fiction

Children's fiction is made up of the wonderful stories that spark imaginations and inspire readers to journey to other times and places through the books they read. From picture books to chapter books, longer novels for older primary children to young adults, there is something for every age and interest. Fiction encompasses the full range of genres: mystery, fantasy, historical, comedy, science fiction, horror and realistic fiction. While children may have a preference, presenting them with opportunities to read stories they might not usually choose opens doors to many new experiences.

New children's fiction is being published every week. This wealth of high-quality books gives every child the ability to find a story that sings to them. The job is far from finished, but the collection of diverse books available is always increasing. Many agents and publishers actively seek out authors who tell their own authentic stories. Author Elle McNicoll has established the Adrien Prize to champion books that include positive depictions of disability. Lists like this will help teachers and pupils find just the right book.

Contemporary children's literature reflects children's lives now. They are stories full of relatable situations and characters. Modern technology and references to current trends or events draw readers into the story with elements they understand. Modern protagonists resonate with children – they want to be like them and share their experiences. When issues of the time are described, children engage eagerly (Heap, 2022a). A strong example of this is books by A.M. Dassu, where issues of identity, respect, community and empowerment are shared honestly in meaningful realistic fiction.

Alongside these modern stories are classics that have stood the test of time: *Winnie the Pooh*, *Treasure Island*, *Anne of Green Gables*, *The Lion, the Witch and the Wardrobe*, and so many more. Full of rich language and gripping adventures, they are timeless. The power of these unforgettable characters pulls children in again and again.

Chartered librarian Veronica Price says, 'The potential for a book to become a classic is hard to define. Character and plot obviously are factors, but some authors have that ability to speak to the heart of a reader which ensures that their books will be passed through generations' (Price, 2023).

That ability to 'speak to the heart of the reader' is precisely why classics continue to earn their place on our classroom shelves, but holding on to those books thoughtfully means being mindful that some classic texts include words or descriptions that, although considered appropriate or a part of everyday language at the time of writing, are now inappropriate, stereotypical or even racist. Rather than throwing away these stories, it is important that teachers and parents address this with children. By discussing the culture and language of the time the book was written and how the world has changed, children will become aware of the development of language and respect for others. It is very important for children to understand and talk about why it is inappropriate to describe groups of people in stereotypical ways, and for adults to help children approach these older texts with sensitivity and awareness. These learning opportunities provide children with a chance to discuss how language evolves over time as inclusiveness, communities and cultures grow (Heap, 2020).

Graphic novels

A graphic novel is a lengthy story told in a comic-strip format. Full-length stories are told through carefully crafted words and illustrations – conveying plot, character development, bold themes and powerful emotions. So much more than a joke and a bit of fun, these high-quality stories often show readers another side of life, building empathy and challenging their view of the world.

Over recent years, graphic novels have risen in popularity among children, teachers and librarians. Despite being considered 'not really reading' by some, graphic novels have proved to be powerful and motivating reading experiences for children.

> I love graphic novels because I like the combination of the words and the pictures. It really helps me to imagine what's going on in the story. They're quick and fun to read. You can go back to reread them lots of times and spot something different every time. Every graphic novel is different. There are classics, adventures and realistic stories. I like the realistic stories the best because I like to read about kids like me.
>
> **Lucy, aged 12 (cited in Heap, 2022b)**

Graphic novels have long been considered the ugly ducklings of 'proper' books. Richard Ruddick runs a graphic novel club with his primary class. The title of his blog – *They Don't Count as Reading* – nails their unfortunate reputation, but running the club tells a different story. Ruddick comments:

> Graphic novels have helped make reading less daunting and more achievable for many less confident readers. Simultaneously, more confident readers have loved having the opportunity to explore texts that have often been suggested as beneath them or not proper reading. The format has something to offer every reader and there is an excellent range of diverse stories that represent all walks of life. Seeing themselves represented in reading hasn't always been possible for some children but they are now much more confident in finding a text that shows their life.
>
> **Ruddick (2023)**

A good place to start is Richard Ruddick's Graphic Novel Padlet (see 'Further reading'), a colourful, constantly updated list of recommendations for primary schools. There really is something for everyone on it; even the most hesitant reader won't be able to resist.

Non-fiction

Children's non-fiction is made up of a collection of factual texts written with the intention to recount, inform, instruct, explain, persuade or discuss. These texts may be read in many different formats, including books, brochures, newspapers, recipes, instruction leaflets and, increasingly, online. To engage positively, pupils must learn to identify purpose, point of view and bias. They need to understand the language and text structures of various types of non-fiction and be able to identify fact versus opinion.

Non-fiction texts open up the whole world for children. For some, what they see in books may be their only experience of what lies outside their local area while, for others, these books may build on the foundations of their awareness of what is going on in the world. We are living in an information-rich, fast-paced, scientific world. Developing solid general knowledge and an understanding of current events is key to becoming a contributing member of society who is thoughtful and aware. Reading non-fiction will help children develop the core knowledge they need and broaden their understanding of what is going on in their local area, nationally and internationally – in the past, present and into the future.

Technical vocabulary is incredibly important as children encounter information about a whole host of modern issues (Heap, 2022a).

Some children may never fall in love with reading stories. It may be reading for purpose that really grabs their interest (see the following section). Children can become avid readers of non-fiction: explanations of how things work, instructions for how to make something really cool, information texts about animals, space or places around the world may grab their attention. They find pleasure in the purpose, which is something to be celebrated.

The Federation of Children's Book Groups, a national charity that aims to bring children and books together, has created an annual celebration of all things factual – National Non-Fiction November (https://fcbg.org.uk/nnfn/). Growing out of National Non-Fiction Day, this month-long event encourages librarians, teachers, parents and, most importantly, children to celebrate information books for younger readers while giving non-fiction books the same recognition as fiction.

Non-fiction should stand alongside fiction on shelves in any primary classroom. It can open doors to history, science and culture in a myriad of accessible and engaging ways, and recent years have produced a generation of beautiful non-fiction books that grab readers of all ages with bright, graphic design. Erin Hamilton, children's librarian for Suffolk Libraries and vice-chair of the Federation of Children's Book Groups, says:

> Non-fiction books should form a vital part of every child's reading experience. These books open up the worlds of history, science, culture and others in engaging and accessible ways. Non-fiction books do not need to be read cover to cover but can be dipped into as per each reader's interest. Many children find non-fiction books fascinating and the books published in today's market are highly visual and appealing to readers of all ages.
>
> **Hamilton (2024)**

Hamilton makes an excellent point here that is worth remembering: we do not have to read these books from cover to cover. This is key for how we stock them and use them in the classroom. So often they are treated as something to be dipped into for a research task. Instead, they should be embraced when children just want to indulge their curiosity. It's OK to pick up a book, flick to what catches their eye, put it down and pick another up tomorrow.

Reading for purpose

As much as we desire children to read for pleasure, we must also teach them to read effectively for purpose. Our aim is for them to become as proficient in reading non-fiction as they are in reading fiction. This is why it is essential that non-fiction forms a central part of a school's reading-for-pleasure initiative, is shared as class read-aloud books and is given status as a quality reading experience. Reading for purpose using non-fiction is a necessary skill across the curriculum. Whether it's science, geography, history or religious education, the ability to read, understand and evaluate facts underpins all aspects of learning.

When designing the reading curriculum, teachers and English leaders must ensure that quality non-fiction is included. Rather than presenting pupils with a series of made-up texts, aim to use real books and extracts that are well-written and prompt thinking and questioning. There is a variety of excellent non-fiction available for children including children's newspapers, encyclopaedias, magazines and websites.

Whether it's reading to gain an in-depth understanding of a topic or to scan for specific information, reading for purpose requires a set of strategies that must be taught and practised if they are to become natural. Regular practice and sharing tips like those listed below will help children become confident and efficient in their reading.

- **Skimming:** Used to gain an overall understanding of the text. Children do not need to read every word, or even every line. They run through the text identifying key words, phrases and headings.
- **Scanning:** Used to identify relevant facts and information quickly. Children read every line at speed, picking out key information.
- **Careful reading:** Used to gain a thorough understanding of the text. Children read every word while self-checking for comprehension. They may wish to use a highlighter to mark important words and phrases. After reading, they may go back and review what they've read, thinking about what they've learned and identifying any further questions.

These purposeful reading strategies give children a toolkit for meeting any text with intention. This toolkit gets picked up willingly only by children who already enjoy reading enough to want to read well. Sue Williamson MBE, a trustee of The Reading Agency, puts this neatly: 'It's only when you read for pleasure, that reading for purpose becomes effortless' (Williamson, 2023).

Poetry

Poetry is a place to escape. With the power to transform the way readers see the world, poetry can provide peace, inspiration and focus. Children enjoy poetry for so many different reasons. They are able to explore language while gaining an awareness of words and their meaning. The musicality of poetry builds a sense of rhythm while developing emotional intelligence. Poems may be silly, funny or scary. They might address loss, remembrance, hope or joy. So much is expressed in so few words, making them much more accessible than full novels. When reading a poem, children bring their own thoughts, experiences and emotions to the meaning, making them intensely personal. Giving children the opportunity to learn poems helps them find out more about themselves and the world around them (Heap, 2021).

Some teachers tend to shy away from teaching poetry. It may be that they don't feel confident teaching it, they've had a bad experience with it at school themselves or the curriculum is just so full that it gets dropped. Some also assume the same reluctance will arise in their classes; that poetry will feel too 'literary' or too abstract for the pupils who already struggle with reading. Sam Creighton, a teacher and literacy lead, has found the exact opposite to be true. Because a poem has 'laser focus on a specific moment / idea / feeling,' he argues (Creighton, 2020), it is often the children who do not see themselves as readers or writers who come into their own with it, and the confidence they build there acts as a springboard into longer texts.

That is reason enough to make space for poetry in the week. With the right poems and the right tools, poetry can broaden children's reading horizons and unlock their imaginations, particularly for those we might least expect to enjoy it.

The Reading for Pleasure pedagogy

The 'Teachers as Readers' study by the Open University and UK Literacy Association, and other Open University studies, have informed the Reading for Pleasure pedagogy (Figure 2.1). It encompasses four key practices: reading aloud; informal book talk and recommendations; and independent reading time, all within a highly social reading environment (Open University, b).

The Reading for Pleasure pedagogy encourages schools to follow the acronym LIST to keep key concepts in mind:

- Learner-led
- Informal
- Social and supported by
- Texts that tempt.

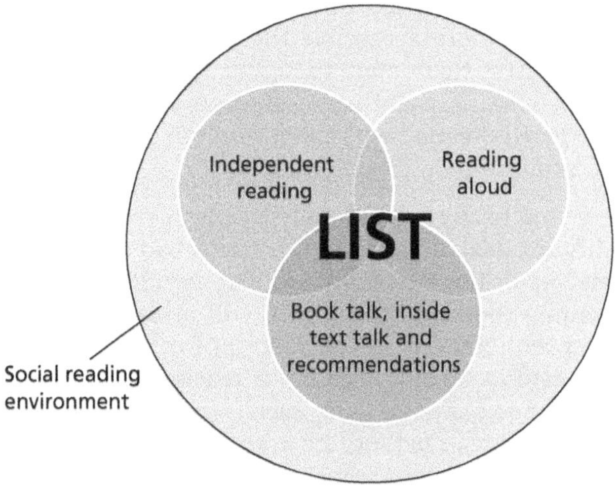

▲ **Figure 2.1 Reading for Pleasure pedagogy (Open University, Reading for Pleasure)**

A reading-rich culture does not just happen by chance. It must be explicitly planned for and modelled by enthusiastic teachers who strive to develop their own knowledge of quality children's literature and of their readers' abilities and needs.

See 'Further reading' for details of the Open University's Reading for Pleasure pedagogy.

Social reading environments

Within a social reading environment, children are immersed in books. They have access to a carefully selected, age-appropriate, diverse and engaging collection of books. Teachers and peers make recommendations and genuine book talk is a regular occurrence.

These reading spaces should be comfortable, not cluttered or overwhelming. Time to chat about books, consider options and read without pressure will help pupils to associate reading and books with positive feelings and a calming sense of safety. This may be in a school library, a classroom library or by a smaller bookshelf.

It is essential that a variety of books is available, including fiction, graphic novels, non-fiction and poetry. These books must be inclusive, diverse and up to date. There is a place for classics, but watch out for stereotypes, racism and stories that are no longer helpful or relevant (see under the 'Fiction' heading of the 'Text types and author's purpose' section earlier in this chapter for suggestions on how to deal with this).

Displays should be engaging and interactive, reflecting pupils' reading journeys with authors they recognise and books they have enjoyed together, as well as 'texts that tempt' for future reads.

Reading aloud

Reading aloud allows children to be carried away by story. It provides access to rich and challenging texts that they may not be able to read themselves. This shared experience gives the class opportunities to discuss plot, characters and themes in engaging book talk. There is nothing quite as powerful as a group of children hanging on a teacher's every word, only to be left on a cliffhanger at the end of the session. Groans and 'just one more chapter' ring out as the book is closed. When teachers know their class and children's literature well, the result is magical.

When reading aloud to pupils, it is important that the teacher has already read the book or is very familiar with it. Not only should they consider whether it will match the interests of the class and provide them with a broad reading experience, but they must also know the themes of the story, difficult plot points and any issues that may have an impact on specific pupils. Teachers need to consider how to direct their reading sessions, when to pause for a question or discussion and know how characters develop. Reading aloud is a bit like a performance – you are enjoying the book together, but the teacher is also using their voice to portray characters, build suspense, enhance emotion and entertain.

Some will argue that with already large workloads, teachers do not have time to pre-read every book. If this is the case, they must rely on solid recommendations from reading experts – people they trust to suggest high-quality books and provide enough detail about potential triggers that they won't find themselves in a difficult situation mid-book. This may be the reading lead at school, reading advisors from the local authority, librarians or bookshop staff, reading consultants or one of the many children's book reviewers who share new books on their blogs and across social media.

Some teachers love to discover a book with their class. They've heard it's great and want to experience those gasp-filled moments and heart-stopping cliffhangers right along with the pupils. This can be a reckless strategy. There is a real risk of stumbling into something that could be upsetting for a pupil – a recent bereavement or family breakdown, the loss of a pet or a medical issue – there are so many individual circumstances to be considered. Only the teacher knows exactly what will be appropriate for their class. This is not to say that books with issues should be avoided, but with prior knowledge and thoughtful preparation the teacher will be able to make careful choices, handle the topic sensitively and build empathy in other children. Appraising a book ahead of time also ensures it is high quality, devoid of any stereotypes, racism or outdated ideas, lends itself to being read aloud and, simply, is not boring.

Reading aloud provides a strong model for pupils' independent reading. Fluency, voice and pacing show children different ways a text can sound and give them something to copy in their own reading. What if a teacher isn't confident reading aloud or feels stuck in monotone expression? It doesn't hurt to practise reading a bit of the story before sharing it with pupils – especially when wanting to do voices. Watch others or ask someone to listen in and provide feedback. Using audiobooks as models is another way to hear a variety of voices. Perhaps the class can work on reading aloud together, identifying the features of a good-quality read aloud. An older class buddying with a younger class gives everyone an opportunity to practise their fluency and expression.

A list generated by the X (formerly Twitter) children's book community highlights that great books to read aloud have:

- manageable chapter lengths or logical stopping points
- pace
- tension building and releasing at key moments
- suspenseful cliffhangers
- a surprising plot twist
- fascinating characters
- opportunities for voices
- action-packed scenes

- a mystery / something to solve / unexpected revelations / light-bulb moments
- humour
- emotion
- opportunities to develop empathy
- ambitious vocabulary.

Reading aloud to children gives them access to many books they may not pick up themselves – because the book is too difficult, they don't think it looks interesting or perhaps they think it's too young for them because it's a picture book. Reading together broadens children's life experiences, raises aspirations and allows them to enjoy some truly great books.

There is no underestimating the power of a picture book. From Reception right through to Year 6 and beyond, so many of these beautiful books speak to readers of all ages, and everyone can take something different from their pages. Their shorter length provides opportunity for discussion, rereading and linking books with similar themes.

The publisher Barrington Stoke creates outstanding books for reading aloud. Funny, touching, empathetic and powerful, they are shorter in length than more typical novels but are bursting with content.

Independent reading

Independent reading is a natural progression from and accompaniment to being read to in class, as pupils are able to emulate adults and become empowered through their book choices. Children's lives have become increasingly full. They are rushed from home to school, to after-school activities, mealtimes and then to bed. The additional appeal of screens means less time is spent reading. Teachers are able to fill this gap by providing purposeful, focused and enjoyable independent reading sessions at school.

Whether you call it DEAR (Drop Everything And Read), ERIC (Everyone Reading In Class) or some other catchy acronym, independent reading must move beyond a routine or filler activity to a meaningful time of authentic reader engagement. Provide pupils with choice, make personal recommendations and give them time to reflect on and share what they have read.

It may be tempting to use this time to complete all those little jobs that need to be done, but seeing a teacher sit down and read is a powerful model for pupils. Enjoy your book and the book chat that follows.

The role of informal book talk

When teachers create meaningful reading experiences, book talk will be a natural result. However, teachers can enhance the frequency and quality of this chat by intentionally implementing book-talk strategies. Opportunities for both child-to-child and adult-to-child interactions will deepen readers' understanding of what they have read, prompt book recommendations and create a positive buzz in school around reading.

Helping children find their next book is a bit like matchmaking. Knowledge of the pupils as readers, as well as an awareness of the high-quality children's literature available in school, is invaluable for teachers to allow them to make those perfect connections. With regular book talk and peer recommendations, the cycle of book selection will be even more successful.

The rights of the reader

Among all this book chat and sharing stories, it's important that the 'rights of the reader' are always placed at the forefront. In the book of the same name created by French educationalist and writer Daniel Pennac and illustrated by the legendary Quentin Blake (2006), the 10 rights of the reader make it clear that the reader is the one in control. They have the right not to finish a book and the right to reread a book as many times as they want. They have the right to skip pages, to read out loud and, most importantly, to read anything they wish. Explore these rights with pupils to discover how they feel about their rights as a reader.

CLPE: 'What We Know Works'

Visit the website of the Centre for Literacy in Primary Education (CLPE) to read 'Reading for Pleasure: What We Know Works', which details its 10 proven strategies for building reading for pleasure (see 'Further reading').

Engaging with authors

Engaging with current and active children's authors and illustrators is a powerful way to promote reading for pleasure. It allows children to interact with positive literary role models, and inspires spoken language, reading and writing skills. The following sections suggest several easy ways to make contact and bring authors into the classroom.

Write to them

Many children's authors love to hear from young readers and will often write back, sometimes sending postcards, bookmarks or posters. Children may ask questions, share ideas or send their own writing and drawings. If an author is happy to be approached, you can usually find their contact details on their website or through their publisher.

Look at websites and newsletters

An author's website is an excellent place to find out more about the author, their inspiration for writing and resources to accompany their books. You may find a goldmine of ideas about how other teachers have used their books. You'll also be able to find out about other books by the same author to take pupils' reading further.

When visiting an author's website, be sure to sign up for their newsletter. This will mean you are among the first to hear about events, new publications and resources linked to their books.

Communicate on social media

Many authors and illustrators are very active on X, Instagram and other platforms. It is a quick and easy way to ask a question or share what has been happening in your classroom. You may find that the author replies with an encouraging message or shares your post with others. Relaying these messages back to pupils is empowering for them as they realise they've been heard and appreciated by someone they admire. Some teachers run an X account just for their class, which they use solely for sharing their classroom activities and communicating with authors. However, always be mindful of your school safeguarding policy and do not share photos of children online.

Contact your local school library services

Your local school library service is an excellent port of call for information about authors. It may be able to provide a list of suitable authors; links to websites and online resources; book boxes containing books by a particular author or group of similar authors; and contact details for authors themselves. It will be able to advise on how to promote authors in the classroom or school library, and is often able to provide schools with details of upcoming author visits and events, perhaps even offering them for a reduced cost.

Plan an author visit

Nothing is more powerful than meeting an author in person. With a school author visit, children are able to listen to a skilled storyteller and ask their own questions. Author visits are incredibly inspiring, as children see how an ordinary person has used their writing skills to share their ideas with the world.

After the author's presentation, there is usually an opportunity to purchase a book and have it signed by the author. That brief, one-to-one chat can be so encouraging.

Author visits may be booked through your school library service, the author's website, publishers or via the Authors Aloud UK website (https://authorsalouduk.co.uk).

In recent years, many authors have been offering online 'visits' too. A video call or webinar can bring the author right into your classroom, up close and personal, for a powerful small-group experience.

Participate in local book awards

There are countless book award schemes around the country every year. Some school library services run local awards and encourage school groups to become involved in nominations, book reviews, voting and the awards ceremony itself. These events offer tremendous opportunities for children to read a range of books, discuss, reflect, vote and have their opinions heard. Attending the awards ceremony gives children the chance to hear from a group of diverse authors, meet them and have their books autographed.

It is also possible for pupils to be involved in larger book events such as the Laugh Out Loud Awards (the Lollies).

National book awards, past and present, such as the Blue Peter Book Awards, the Lollies Book Awards, Waterstones Children's Book Prize, Costa Children's Book Awards, the Yoto Carnegie Medals for Writing and for Illustration (Kate Greenaway Medal) and the Guardian Children's Fiction Prize provide useful lists of high-quality books to explore with your class.

Attend local events and literary festivals

Every year there are many local literary events: local library workshops, school library services events and literary festivals. Sometimes there will be weekday events for schools before a weekend festival begins. If possible, take your class or encourage them to attend with their families. Often the weekend workshops are free of charge and very family friendly.

A quick internet search for 'children's literary festivals' will show you what is happening around the country and near you.

Find a school patron of reading

Some schools are fortunate to have a school patron of reading. This is a special relationship with an author or illustrator in which the professional supports the reading programme of the school, provides inspiration for the pupils and promotes reading for pleasure. Enquire about a patron of reading through the Patron of Reading website (www.patronofreading.co.uk).

Enter competitions and request sample chapters

If you are active on X or Instagram, and follow authors, publishers and booksellers, watch out for competitions and special offers. There are often competitions to win a book for your class. This creates a buzz around an author and eager anticipation of a new book.

Listen to podcasts

There are podcasts on almost every topic imaginable. Education podcasts are current, interesting and an easy way to stay up to date with authors, new publications and ideas for your classroom. Listen at home, on your commute or in your classroom while doing prep. Some podcasts are appropriate for children, so you can share them with your class.

Podcasts are available by searching the internet or via various apps such as the Podcast app, Audible, iTunes, Spotify, Google Podcasts and Apple Podcasts.

Interviews with authors are a great way to hear from the authors themselves and be inspired to try new ideas. Try *Down the Rabbit Hole*, *In the Reading Corner*, *The Teachers' Podcast*, *Fun Kids Book Worms* and *Library Girl and Book Boy*.

Contact local bookshops

Try speaking to your local independent bookstore or chain. It will have links with a variety of authors and make recommendations about which may be the best fit for your school. If an author is visiting the shop for a book signing or workshop, it may be possible to take pupils along to the event or plan a school author visit while they are in the area.

Other ideas

You could try VIP Reading, which is a book-selection resource for parents and schools (see www.vipreading.co.uk/schools), arrange a visit to an illustrator's studio or follow X book clubs / chats / read-alongs.

Teachers as readers

A teacher can have a powerful influence on a pupil's life. When that teacher is an enthusiastic reader who models and shares their reading experiences, they will have a positive impact on pupils' own desire to read and the frequency of their reading at home and at school. It is only with first-hand knowledge of a book that a teacher can make a genuine recommendation; children can tell the difference between 'I think you'd love this' and 'this got good reviews'. But being a reader privately is only half the job. Pupils need to *see* you reading; to watch you laugh at a book, hear you complain about one, catch you halfway through something on your desk at lunchtime. In *Reading for Pleasure: 100 Ideas for Primary Teachers*, Scott Evans argues that giving pupils 'a glimpse into your literary life inside and outside school' helps them learn not only about you but about themselves as readers (Evans, 2023). A pupil who sees their teacher as a real reader gets permission to see themselves as one too.

This does not mean the teacher needs to read every new children's book published and spend all their time reading. However, keeping up with current publications, knowing what is popular, being aware of contentious books or authors and reading some of what you are offering pupils is important for making genuine recommendations.

The impact and benefits of reading for pleasure

There's no question there is a positive relationship between reading for pleasure and attainment in reading. The more children read, the better readers they become. In 2012, the Department for Education found several benefits of reading for pleasure, sharing them in the report 'Research evidence on reading for pleasure' (DfE, 2012).

The DfE report highlighted that the case for reading for pleasure is backed by a substantial body of research. Since a review published by Clark and Rumbold in 2006, studies such as PIRLS (Progress in International Reading Literacy Study) 2006 (Mullis et al, 2007) and the PISA 2009 survey internationally, as well as research by the National Literacy Trust, have continued to demonstrate that children who enjoy reading read more, and achieve higher reading test scores. Overall, evidence indicates that reading for pleasure can lead to gains in attainment, vocabulary, general knowledge, reading attitudes and social and emotional development.

If reading for pleasure is central to your pedagogy, it will affect your wider approach to English lessons. Carrying the same diligence into choosing rich, varied, compassionate, empathy-building texts will let you push children's developing love of reading towards word reading, fluency and comprehension. Reading for pleasure isn't an intervention; it's the environment within which all reading develops.

Reading for empathy

Empathy is being able to understand or imagine the feelings of others when we haven't experienced the same ourselves. Reading for empathy includes being able to name and recognise feelings, looking at things from another perspective, building links between individuals or communities, welcoming diversity, listening to other people's stories and taking action to make the world a better place. These aspects might be developed through books following key themes such as cultural celebrations, SEND, war and refuge, poverty or loss. Intentionally developing children's ability to read for empathy will contribute to the building of a more compassionate, united society.

Founded in 2014, EmpathyLab (www.empathylab.uk) believes in the power of reading to build real-life empathy skills. Helping children develop empathy is more important than ever as the world continues to change and present new challenges.

EmpathyLab has developed four key programmes:

1 **Empathy Day:** Held every June since 2017, Empathy Day is all about helping children develop their empathy for others and gain understanding of different experiences and situations. The day focuses on using books to step into someone else's shoes. The more children empathise with characters, the more they are able to understand the world around them and empathise with other people. Empathy Day is followed up later in the year with Empathy Action Month in November. Children have the opportunity to consider empathy's power to influence social change.
2 **Schools programme:** EmpathyLab offers CPD for individual teachers as well as an affiliate schools programme. This allows teachers or schools to explore the research behind EmpathyLab in greater depth

and place empathy at the heart of their school ethos. It encompasses reading for pleasure, wellbeing, social activism and school culture.

3 **Read for Empathy book collections:** Each year, EmpathyLab brings together a collection of books suitable for children aged 3–16. These books are chosen for their empathy-building power. They can be used by teachers and parents to help children develop new perspectives, name and share emotions, gain insights into other ways of life and understand how people might feel in certain circumstances. The primary and secondary collections are accompanied by guidebooks that highlight each book and provide tips and activities for using the books with children (see 'Further reading').
4 **Links with authors and illustrators:** EmpathyLab has gathered a team of children's authors and illustrators who support its mission. Through interviews, book recommendations, short stories, empathy activities and reading aloud, these inspirational authors and illustrators model the power of stories for building empathy.

Reading in action: instructional strategies

There are so many wonderful ideas for promoting reading for pleasure in your classroom. The Open University Reading for Pleasure website (see 'Further reading') and keen members of the education community on X and Instagram regularly share techniques to try with your class.

Making recommendations

Helping children choose a quality book

The children's book community on X regularly chats about how to make quality recommendations for children. The following list is a compilation of one of those chats (Boddington et al, 2020).

Recommend:

- a book they will love
- a book that will make them laugh
- a book that inspires
- a book that shows a different culture
- a book that excites
- a book they can see themselves in (representing where they are from, their situation or the type of person they are)

- a book that takes them away from reality
- a book that makes them feel (e.g. experiencing sadness then finding happiness again)
- great stories that will help them to become even better people through empathy and understanding.

Teacher recommendations

Jon Biddle, primary teacher and advocate of reading for pleasure, leaves sticky notes on books recommending them to certain pupils. He explains, 'There's visible excitement when they get handed the book or notice it on their desk, and it does so much for the "reading relationship"' (Biddle, 2023). It takes barely any time to do this, yet it communicates something very powerful: that an adult has taken the time to think about you personally and choose a book they think you will enjoy. For children who don't view themselves as readers, that personal recommendation can be all they need.

'What are you reading?'

Create a small, changeable display with the titles or covers of the books the teacher and other adults in the classroom are currently reading. This will have the most impact if they are children's books, but it's a great model to share adult books, magazines and other reading materials too. Seeing their teachers as readers embeds the idea that reading is a lifelong activity.

Peer recommendations

Whether it's casual book chat, children leaving a short sticky-note review on the front cover of a book or a more formal book review, book recommendations from other children can be some of the most powerful motivators to read. Once a class is raving about a book, it will fly off the shelf and develop a lengthy waiting list.

Pupil recommendation shelves

Jon Biddle takes his sticky-note strategy one step further with pupil-recommendation shelves. Each week, two pupils work together to choose a selection of books to recommend to the class. For each book, they write the reason they recommend it on a sticky note and fix it to the front of the book. The pair are given an opportunity to talk to the rest of the class about their choices, which makes their selections very popular.

Julia Bichard, librarian at the Guille-Allès Library in Guernsey, suggests making peer-recommendation bookmarks (Bichard, 2022). Readers can fill them in quickly and easily, then leave them for other children to discover.

Book show and tell

Each week, reserve time for a few pupils to 'show and tell' one of their favourite books. This could be a current favourite or one they've loved for years. They can show the book, share illustrations and talk about why they've enjoyed it. A collection of sentence stems would help less confident speakers plan what to say (for example 'I love this book because…', 'It taught me…', 'My favourite character is ___ because…'). Children may bring the book from home or choose one from the class or school library. Be mindful of pupils who may not have a large selection of books at home, and help them select something special from school.

Book newsletter

A school or class reading newsletter gives pupils an opportunity to share short book reviews. Look at publications such as *The Week Junior* or *Toppsta* for examples of what an effective review looks like.

Deputy headteacher and reading specialist Dean Boddington has created a whole-school reading newsletter for pupils, parents and teachers, entitled 'No Shelf Control', which he shares freely with other schools (see 'Further reading'). It contains Q&As with authors, details of new and upcoming books and book collections based on themes. Using this as a model for sharing books in your own school will allow pupils to make personal recommendations and build excitement around books.

Reading scrapbooks

A new take on the class mascot that goes home with a different child each week, reading scrapbooks bring families into the celebration of reading. When it's a pupil's turn to take the scrapbook home, they complete a double-page spread about a book they've read recently. They fill the pages with everything they love about the book including extracts, illustrations, reasons they enjoyed it and why they think others should read it.

Recommended reading lists

- **The Reader Teacher, Scott Evans:** The Reader Teacher website (www.thereaderteacher.com) contains up-to-date recommended-reading lists organised by year group and key stage. There are Monthly Must-

Reads celebrating new books, and #BookMatch posters that point readers towards books similar to those by their favourite authors.

- **Read for Empathy Collections:** Produced annually since 2017, the Read for Empathy Book Collections (www.empathylab.uk/RFE) are carefully curated lists of books that challenge readers, reaching right into their hearts and minds. Each book addresses a challenge or topic children need to be familiar with to understand their own lives better or the lives of others.
- **Books for Topics:** The Books for Topics website (www.booksfortopics.com) contains lists of high-quality books for children. They are organised by topic, age and season, including national curriculum topics.
- **Toppsta:** The Toppsta website (https://toppsta.com) provides children with opportunities to read book reviews written by other children and adults who love children's literature. Children may add their own reviews of books they've read and enter competitions to win free books.
- **CLPE:** The Centre for Literacy in Primary Education provides lists of high-quality books organised by theme, author and topic, as well as staff picks (https://clpe.org.uk/books/booklists). Categories such as 'Girl Detectives', 'Human Rights Day' and books inspired by Mary Shelley and *Frankenstein* help readers to make links between so many different books.
- **Dean Boddington's Tube Maps:** In the style of London Underground maps, Dean Boddington's Reading for Pleasure Tube Maps (Boddington, 2020) help children and teachers make links between books. If children have enjoyed books by a particular author, they can follow the same-coloured line on the Tube Map to find something similar. If you enjoyed *Beast Quest*, try *The Land of Roar* by Jenny McLachlan. If you enjoyed the *Rainbow Magic* series, try the *Starfell* series by Dominique Valente.
- **Ashley Booth:** Teacher Ashley Booth has created lists of 100 books to read in each stage of primary school – key stage 1, Years 3–4 and Years 5–6 (Booth, 2017). These lists contain newer books as well as some classics.

Not every book will grab every reader, and that's OK. The right book is different for every child. It's incredibly rewarding to provide children with a range of reading experiences to work out their reading preferences and help them find their reading spark.

Informal book talk

Whether it's spontaneous or prompted by the teacher, talking about books is at the heart of a classroom where reading is valued and enjoyed. It comes from a genuine enthusiasm for books and will grow as pupils practise sharing what they have read and listening to others.

Book tasting café

Encourage pupils to try new books by setting up a book tasting café. This can be as elaborate or as simple as you wish. Invite pupils into a restaurant-style set-up, complete with menus and tablecloths. The centrepiece for each table is a basket of intriguing books. Each table should have a different type of book (for example picture books, poetry, non-fiction, graphic novels, historical novels) or theme (for example friendship, animals, aliens, war, STEM).

Ask pupils to choose a book to sample. After they've read a few pages, they should complete some question prompts on their menu, jot down any new vocabulary on their place mat and record on a bookmark the title / author of any books they particularly enjoy.

For the next course, move the baskets of books around the tables and repeat the activity. By the end of the session, pupils will have tasted a number of different books and will hopefully have a list of new books they want to read. Ask them to reflect on how the experience made them feel and jot it down on their napkins.

Inviting parents / carers to join in with a book tasting will allow children to try a greater range of books, prompt valuable book chat between adults and children and help to develop a school community of readers. Often parents only see the books for sale on supermarket shelves. Showing them some of the wide range of high-quality literature available will help them to make positive choices for their children (Literacy with Miss P, 2018a).

Question of the week

Much of the discussion around books we see in primary classrooms takes place within the context of a reading lesson – for example, in a comprehension task, with an answer in mind, under time constraints. That has value, certainly, but it also sends the message that talking about books is something you do academically, rather than something you do because you want to.

Teacher Cassie Hayward-Tapp, who teaches Year 6 and is English lead in her primary school, has designed a whole-class routine that creates space for just this sort of talk. Every Monday, she puts up a reading-related question in her classroom book corner, deliberately not a comprehension question but something open, about personal experience, preference or reflection. Children write their answers on sticky notes, which go up beside the question over the course of the week; answers are read and shared in class; on Friday they all come down, and a new question goes up on the following Monday. Cassie has created a bank of questions that she's made available for free on the *TES* resources website, so the routine can be copied and pasted into any teacher's repertoire (Hayward-Tapp, 2021).

Example questions include:

- If you could give a piece of advice to one character, who would it be and what would you say?
- Who is the author you would most like to meet and why?
- What is a fact you have learned from a non-fiction book?

These types of questions may also be used in whole-school or key-stage assemblies. Ask a question, encourage the pupils to chat in pairs then share their answers with the group. Making a regular habit of book chat will help children think about and share more of their reading experiences while creating a buzz about books around school.

Class reading history

Find a way to keep track of the books read together as a class; this could be printed covers displayed on the wall or pegged on a string, or the titles added to a list. Give pupils opportunities to reminisce about favourite books and make links between them. Add memories of author visits, special reading events and other book activities, to create a complete picture of your class reading journey.

Jon Biddle asks pupils to work in small groups to complete reading histories at the end of each year. With pictures of book covers and other reading events, pupils create a timeline of their class's year of reading (Biddle, 2023).

Class novel working wall

Teacher Alex Barton suggests creating a class novel working wall. Add the cover of the book and information about the author, leaving space for pupils to add details about the characters, new vocabulary and questions about the plot. 'Children are responsible for updating it and they generate all the ideas,' Alex says. 'We have 5 minute "book talk" time after our 15 minute story time and it works wonders' (Barton, 2023).

Texts of today

At different times throughout the year, put all the pupils' independent reading books together on a table and take a photo. Use this as a prompt to chat about the types of books the class likes, any trends and which books they're hoping to read next. If you'd like to compare with other classes, use #textsoftoday on X to connect with other schools.

Year 6 teacher Richard Ruddick says, 'Texts of today has inspired children to read books they were previously uncertain of. Seeing other classes enjoying them from other schools provides excellent opportunities for discussion and is a fantastic way to access a greater range of peer recommendations' (Ruddick, 2023).

Reading for Pleasure Padlet

Jon Biddle's Reading for Pleasure Padlet (see 'Further reading') is an absolute goldmine of practical reading ideas and resources. From a map of independent children's bookshops to reading surveys, reading awards and more, it is overflowing with ideas to enhance reading provision.

Formal reading teaching

There is no one right way to organise your class for teaching reading. In recent years, whole-class reading has grown in popularity due to the quality of the reading discussion, providing everyone with access to the same text and the teacher being able to give all pupils the same learning experience. This is not to say that group reading should never be used. In mixed-age classes, or in situations where there is a large spread of attainment levels, it may be the correct choice. There should be a rationale as to why the teacher is choosing a specific style of lesson, to ensure it is appropriate and effective. A mix of styles may also work. Depending on the needs of the pupils, one text might be best taught to the whole class while, on another week, group learning might be the best way forwards.

Whole-class reading

Whole-class reading happens when all pupils in the class take part in a reading lesson together with a common shared text – on the interactive whiteboard, on copied sheets or through multiple copies of the actual book. The teacher leads the lesson, focusing on vocabulary, pausing to discuss character, plot and the author's use of language, and challenging pupils to make inferences. There may be oral discussion of key questions or a written element to the session.

Group-guided reading

A more traditional approach to teaching reading, group-guided reading, is often a carousel of reading activities that take place over the course of a week. The class is split into ability groups, with each group having the opportunity to work with the teacher (or another adult) for at least one session each week. Often, groups read differentiated texts based on their reading ability. On days when the group is not working with an adult, pupils may be completing follow-up questions, pre-reading for the next session, reading a related text or doing another reading task.

Child-led groups

Much like a group reading session with an adult, pupils work in small groups to explore a text. The teacher may read the text with the whole class before breaking into groups, or pupils will be given a text to read together. They may read individually before discussing, work in pairs or share the text in a round-robin style. The smaller group size gives more pupils an opportunity to read aloud. After reading the text, there are multiple options for class discussion: pupils may work together to answer questions provided by the teacher, they may come up with their own questions or they might respond to the text through role play, writing or art. Teachers may assign a leader for each group to help keep everyone on track and ensure each pupil gets a chance to share their thoughts. This strategy gives the teacher freedom to move around the groups, listening and dipping in and out of conversations. This way, they are able to pick up on excellent examples of analysis, common misconceptions and tricky vocabulary. A whole-class debrief at the end of the session gives pupils an opportunity to share answers to the questions (with confidence, because they've already discussed them as a group), share insights and talk about what they need to know more about.

Reciprocal reading

Reciprocal reading is a style of child-led group in which pupils take on a leadership role with a specific focus (see, for example, Reading Rockets, 2026c). Pupils take turns to guide the discussion by focusing on different areas of reading, such as summarising, questioning, clarifying, predicting, vocabulary or feelings. The number of roles depends on group size and the objectives of the lesson. Once assigned their role, pupils read a short section of text and highlight or make notes linked to their role, for example:

- Summariser – look for key ideas in this section of text
- Questioner – ask questions about the text
- Predictor – make predictions about what will come next in the text
- Clarifier – look for confusing sections of the text and try to make sense of them.

Next, pupils take turns to share what they've found and involve the rest of the group in a discussion. Before pupils undertake these roles independently, the teacher will model the process and support early attempts.

Encourage active reading

Active reading is approaching a text with purpose, a determination to understand and a focus on its relevance (for example Open University, a). Active reading should be modelled for pupils, with teachers taking time to pause, explain what they're doing and speak their thinking aloud.

Active reading strategies include:

- **Asking questions as you read.** Why was this text written? Who is it for? Focus on the plot, characters or information provided. Teachers can ask these questions aloud and model themselves thinking and coming up with possible answers. 'Perhaps it's this… or maybe it's that…'
- **Underlining or highlighting key words and phrases.** Show pupils how to be selective in this, so they don't end up with an entire page of highlighter!
- **Annotating the text** with key points, links across the text or with other texts, summaries, questions, and so on. If reading from a book, sticky notes may be used.
- **Looking for cohesive devices or signposts** that help you to understand how the text is organised (e.g. 'however', 'on the other hand', 'therefore', 'in conclusion').

Developing fluency

Professor Timothy Rasinski, writing for the Education Endowment Foundation (EEF), describes reading fluency as having three elements:

accuracy, automaticity and prosody (Rasinski, 2022; Figure 3.3). Prosody links reading accuracy with comprehension, allowing children to read with appropriate expression.

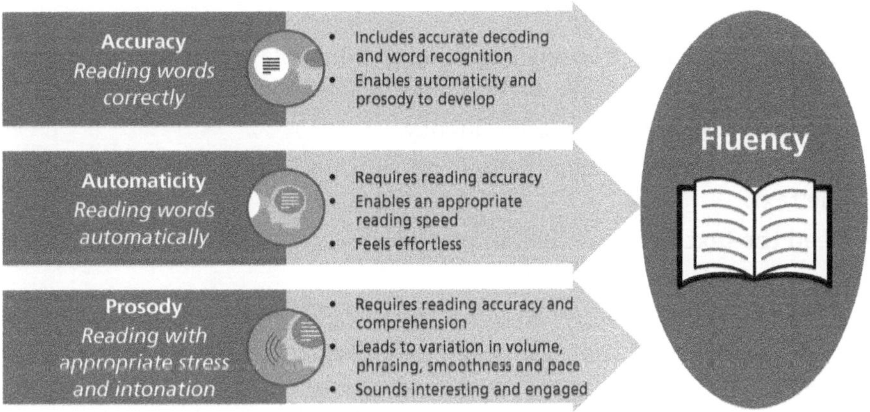

▲ **Figure 2.2 Reading fluency (Education Endowment Foundation, 2021)**

In her EEF blog post, 'Shining a light on reading fluency', assistant headteacher and EEF literacy content specialist, Sarah Green, suggests a fluency scale rubric, like that adapted from Zutell and Rasinski (1991), is a useful tool to support focused development of children's reading fluency. Teachers use the rubric to consider pupils' attainment in terms of expression and volume, phrasing, smoothness and pace, to assess their fluency, identify progress and provide support.

Fluency strategies

There are a number of strategies that can help to build fluency in readers. In each case, it is essential that every pupil is able to see the text, either with a copy of the book, a photocopied passage or the extract displayed on the interactive whiteboard (Reading Rockets, 2026a).

Modelled reading

In modelled reading, the adult reads aloud while children follow along the text. The adult demonstrates effective expression, pacing and phrasing, so children hear what fluent reading sounds like. The aim is for children to internalise and imitate these reading strategies, then use them independently.

Choral reading
Choral reading is the whole class or a group of pupils reading aloud in unison. It builds fluency and confidence, as children are able to listen to others before reading on their own (Reading Rockets, 2026b). Here's how it works:

- Choose a text suited to reading aloud (predictable or repeated patterns, not too long, at the independent reading level for most pupils).
- Read the text aloud to model fluency.
- Encourage pupils to use their finger or a text marker to follow along the text.
- Read the text again with all pupils joining in.

Echo reading
Echo reading occurs when an adult reads a sentence of text, modelling fluency for children. The class, group or individual echoes back the same line with similar pace, phrasing and expression. Children must be able to see the text and read rather than just repeat. The teacher may wish to read the entire text first, so pupils are aware of the content and don't lose understanding through the choppiness of echo reading.

Paired reading
When using paired reading, the teacher strategically pairs pupils to take turns reading. These pairings may consist of more fluent readers with less fluent readers, or equally matched readers working together. In the former case, the more fluent reader goes first, to provide a model for the other. They take turns to read, alternating by sentence, paragraph or page. Pupils may also read together or have one read the entire text while the other listens. They should be taught to give positive feedback and how to gently correct misread words.

Audio-assisted reading
Audio-assisted reading is when children read along with an audiobook or recording of an adult or child reading a text. They try to match the pace, phrasing and expression of the recording before trying to read it on their own. This builds confidence and provides an excellent model for reading.

Reader's Theatre
Reader's Theatre is a fun oral reading strategy involving scripts and parts. These scripts may be purchased, found online or created by the teacher. The best Reader's Theatre scripts have multiple parts and lots of dialogue. Children practise reading their scripts on their own then come together

as a group to focus on fluency and expression. When the time comes to perform, they use teamwork to share their story with the rest of the class (or in assembly). Unlike a play, there are no props or costumes, and the script does not need to be memorised.

Repeated reading

Repeated reading – a method proposed by educational psychologist and reading researcher S. Jay Samuels – occurs when children are given opportunities to reread short passages of text, with the aim of becoming faster and more accurate each time (Samuels, 1979). Texts should be short (about 50–200 words) and challenging for the reader. By repeating the same text, reading becomes more automatic and word knowledge increases (Shanahan, 2017).

What about round-robin reading?

One pupil reading to the rest of the class in a round robin or 'popcorn' style (one child reading at random) does not provide enough reading practice. Children may lose their place, stop listening or be so focused on their upcoming turn that they don't attend to what anyone else is reading. Anxiety may cause children to panic about reading, and very little is taken in. Much more learning takes place when everyone is reading.

Comprehension questions

Many reading lessons are based around the asking and answering of a range of questions. Although the ability to answer questions can reflect children's comprehension of a text, it is important that this is not the only strategy used. High-quality, varied questions should sit alongside opportunities to reflect on what they have read. Start with the power of the text. How does it make children feel? What do they notice? What are the Big Ideas or themes? What does this text mean to them?

Answering comprehension questions often requires children to tap into more than one aspect of reading. To make an inference, they must understand the vocabulary and retrieve information. To make a prediction, they must infer what is going to happen next, based on what they have already read. Teachers must help pupils to make links between these types of questions, to build their overall comprehension. It is because of this that questions should not be taught entirely in isolation. After introducing pupils to strategies to help with retrieval, prediction or understanding vocabulary in context, combining question types will allow them to think more deeply about the text and their understanding of it.

When planning a reading lesson, begin with vocabulary. This may include pre-teaching key words, or directing pupils to use context clues to work out the meaning of unknown words. Once vocabulary is secure, children can dig deeper into text meaning.

Further questions may be organised by type, or be combined to take children through the text with an overall summary question towards the end. One lesson may focus on specific strategies for making inferences by activating background knowledge and finding evidence in the text, while another may look at the figurative language used throughout the passage. The style of the lesson and type of questions used should match the needs of the pupils and the objectives to be taught.

Careful selection of a text is essential, as each will have something different to offer. One may be full of opportunities for inference, while another may be bursting with creative vocabulary that challenges children to search for meaning. Finding a great text where a variety of potential questions leap off the page is like striking gold.

Questions for reading lessons do not all need to be created by the class teacher. This can be time-consuming, and there are many fantastic resources available for whole books and extracts. When choosing published resources, look for those that contain high-quality texts rather than one-off extracts written solely for the purpose of comprehension. Real texts will be more engaging, contain challenge and point children towards a real book they can continue reading.

Not all reading-comprehension lessons need to involve writing. Teachers may wish pupils to practise writing their answers, especially when preparing for assessments, but an oral discussion is equally valuable. Pupils can listen to each other's answers, agree, disagree, build on the response or give a counterargument. Using sentence frames allows children to develop their oracy and think logically about what they want to say. For example, when inferring a character's emotions, they might say, 'I think X is feeling ________ because ________'. This sentence frame prompts the child to give a reason for their inference and look for clues in the text. As this sentence structure becomes automatic, they will be able to use it in written answers as well.

Further reading

Biddle, J., Reading for Pleasure Padlet, https://padlet.com/Jon_Biddle/reading-for-pleasure-woam2an149vg

Boddington, D., 'No Shelf Control', https://misterbodd.wordpress.com/no-shelf-control/

CLPE, 'Choosing and Using Quality Children's Texts: What We Know Works', https://clpe.org.uk/research/choosing-and-using-quality-childrens-texts-what-we-know-works

CLPE, 'Reading for Pleasure: What We Know Works', https://clpe.org.uk/research/reading-pleasure-what-we-know-works

EmpathyLab, Read for Empathy book collections, www.empathylab.uk/RFE

Green, S. (2021) 'Shining a light on reading fluency', https://educationendowmentfoundation.org.uk/news/eef-blog-shining-a-spotlight-on-reading-fluency

Open University, Reading for Pleasure, ourfp.org; specific details of the Reading for Pleasure pedagogy at https://ourfp.org/reading-for-pleasure-pedagogy/

Pennac, D. and Blake, Q. (2006) *The Rights of the Reader*. Walker Books.

Rasinski, T. (2022) 'Why focus on reading fluency?' https://educationendowmentfoundation.org.uk/news/why-focus-on-reading-fluency

Ruddick, R., Graphic Novel Padlet, https://padlet.com/rruddick9zra/graphic-novels-73uh2srzpbia

CHAPTER 3
WRITING

Writing: the Big Ideas

Writing is one of the most powerful things we teach children. Giving every child the confidence to put their thoughts into words, along with the skills to do so clearly, purposefully and with their own voice, is essential for helping them grow into communicators who can share ideas, influence others and make sense of the world around them.

Writing has a huge impact on children's learning across the curriculum. It consolidates knowledge, sharpens thinking, builds vocabulary, reinforces spelling and deepens comprehension, giving children a way of recording what they know and making it their own. Learning to write in primary school is about so much more than handwriting, spelling or using grammar correctly. Pupils are encouraged to make purposeful word choices and build cohesive compositions, while developing their own style and voice as writers. This intricate combination of skills takes time to nurture through modelling, experience and feedback.

Of course, writing does not stand alone. It builds on everything children have been developing in spoken language and reading: the vocabulary and sentence structures rehearsed through talk, and the text types, authorial choices and rhythms of language encountered as readers. If children can say it, they are far more likely to be able to write it; if they have read a strong example of it, they have a model to draw on.

Read more about this in Chapter 1, in the section titled 'Spoken language: the Big Ideas', and Chapter 2, in the section titled 'Reading: the Big Ideas'.

Writing is made up of two elements that work hand in hand to create confident, expressive, independent writers: transcription and composition.

Transcription includes the more technical aspects of writing. Fluent spelling and handwriting become the vehicles for expression. Through knowledge of phonics and spelling, children acquire a bank of words they can spell quickly and accurately. Building on the sound–spelling correspondence of phonics with an understanding of word structure and spelling patterns helps children to make connections between words they already know and new words they would like to use. Alongside this, flowing, legible handwriting allows children to write freely, and focus on what they want to say.

Composition includes all other aspects of writing, from the vocabulary, grammar and punctuation used for sentence building to the structure of paragraphs, knowledge of text types, choices around formality and so much more.

Taken together, transcription and composition encompass the spelling, punctuation, grammar and vocabulary set out in the national curriculum's statutory programmes of study. Rather than treating these as a separate, detachable strand, this book weaves them through the teaching of writing, which is where children meet them in practice and where they most obviously earn their keep.

As with spoken language and reading, Year 1 teachers must carefully consider pupils' progress towards the EYFS Early Learning Goals in Writing. Further development of fine motor skills, letter formation, using phonics for early spelling and a child's understanding of communication in written sentences must be taken into account before tackling the national curriculum.

Building blocks of writing

Handwriting

Handwriting is a core communication skill that has impact across the curriculum. Yes, people are using keyboards more than ever before, but there is still the need to be able to form letters correctly and legibly to share ideas. There are many preferred methods and styles of teaching handwriting. It must be taught explicitly to ensure development of muscle strength, correct pencil grip, letter orientation and formation, as well as letter-joins. Mastering legible, fluent handwriting allows children to turn their attention to the other challenges of writing without being hindered by putting pen to paper.

Phonics

In writing, children use their knowledge of sound–symbol correspondence to write letters that match the sounds they hear in a word. As their knowledge of phonemes (sounds) and graphemes (letters) increases, they are able to build more words with a greater range of spelling patterns.

Spelling

Spelling is using the conventional pattern of letters to form a particular word (including the many exceptions to spelling rules in the English language). Strong spelling knowledge allows children to write fluently and communicate effectively.

Grammar

Grammar is the system and structure of the English language. Its rules help us decide the order of words and which form of a word to use. A lot of our first knowledge of grammar is picked up through spoken language. Teachers help pupils apply this knowledge to writing and make intentional language choices. There is a specific body of grammatical knowledge children are required to learn in primary school, which serves as the basis of coherent, effective writing throughout their lives.

As a part of grammar, words are categorised according to the job they do in a sentence. They may be nouns, verbs, adjectives, adverbs, conjunctions, prepositions, pronouns or determiners. An awareness of these parts of speech allows children to create grammatically correct sentences.

Sentence construction

A sentence is one word or a group of words that form a complete thought – it makes sense on its own. Sentences begin with a capital letter and conclude with appropriate end punctuation (. ? !). Sentence construction can be one of the most difficult aspects of writing for children. They must arrange the words in a manner that is grammatically correct, choose the most effective vocabulary and apply punctuation.

Types of sentences include:

- simple sentence – a sentence made up of one independent clause
- compound sentence – a sentence made up of two independent clauses joined by a co-ordinating conjunction or by a semicolon
- complex sentence – a sentence made up of an independent clause and one (or more) subordinate clauses that begin with subordinating conjunctions.

Punctuation

Punctuation is a set of standardised marks used to clarify meaning. These marks may separate words, phrases or sentences. Correct punctuation guides the reader through the text, providing coherence and structure.

Children gradually build up their knowledge of punctuation as they progress through school and as the different marks become necessary in their writing. Full stops to demarcate sentences come first, with question marks, commas, apostrophes and others following. An understanding of the function of each punctuation mark, along with clear modelling, will help children use them securely.

Paragraphs

Writers use paragraphs to sequence sentences cohesively to develop ideas. These sentences are related to the same topic and organised in a logical order. A paragraph often begins with a topic sentence that briefly explains what the paragraph is about. It may end with a short conclusion or summary sentence.

Within and between paragraphs, sentences are linked with cohesive devices (words and phrases that tie ideas together smoothly, creating a coherent piece of writing).

Text types

Text types are different styles of writing categorised by their purpose, language features and structure. Not all writing fits neatly into one text type, but having an awareness of different types of writing will help children organise their ideas and write with clear intent. The 'Writing in action' section later in this chapter looks at how to teach text types in practice, organised by the purposes children write for.

The National Literacy Trust's 'A guide to text types: narrative, non-fiction and poetry' offers a fuller breakdown of structural and language features for each type:

Table 3.1 Guide to text types (National Literacy Trust, 2013)

Narrative	Non-fiction	Poetry
Adventure	Discussion texts	Free verse
Mystery	Explanatory texts	Visual poems
Science fiction	Instructional texts	Structured poems
Fantasy	Persuasion texts	Narrative poems
Historical fiction	Non-chronological reports	
Contemporary fiction	Recounts	
Dilemma stories		
Dialogue		
Play scripts		
Film narratives		
Myths		
Legends		
Fairy tales		
Fables		
Traditional tales		

Phonics and spelling

Phonics

Phonics is one of the pillars of the English language – the very first building blocks of how we say, read and write words. Children will begin their phonics journey in Nursery and Reception (some even earlier if they begin to explore sounds at home). It is essential that schools follow an approved phonics scheme and teachers work together to provide an engaging programme that allows pupils to progress. This progress should be tracked, so that any gaps are identified and addressed quickly.

Once children are secure in using phonics for both reading and writing, they will be ready to move on to spelling and an exploration of the many patterns of the English language.

Spelling

Spelling is so much more than a list of words and a weekly test. It is teaching pupils to understand the sometimes complex set of rules that govern how we put letters together to form words. There are patterns and exceptions that need to be learned through practice, memory and understanding. The ultimate aim is for children to be able to apply their spelling knowledge in their day-to-day writing.

When it comes to the teaching of spelling patterns, there are numerous schemes that may be followed. The best starting point is the spelling appendix for the national curriculum (DfE, 2013a). This document makes clear the expectations for each year group with example words and guidance.

In addition to regular spelling patterns, children must also learn to spell 'sight words', also known as 'common exception words'. These are words that do not follow a usual spelling pattern but appear regularly when reading and writing. Because phonics will not help when working out the spelling of these words, different strategies must be used.

When children write, they need to draw on their knowledge of known words, common letter strings, word structures and word meaning. Modelling this thought process will help them to make connections between words and spot familiar patterns. Regularly revisiting spellings through retrieval practice will consolidate learning in their long-term memory.

Readers as writers

The best writers in any given class will invariably be readers. Pie Corbett, the creator of the Talk for Writing approach, simply states: 'Ask any author what advice they have for someone who wants to be a writer and they always say the same thing: "Read, read, read." The reading makes the writer' (Corbett, 2008). Corbett goes on to explain how children who struggle to write creatively aren't short of ideas; they simply haven't had access to the building blocks of language with which to develop their ideas – and that access comes from reading. Children who are exposed to a wide range of reading, and are read to regularly, will almost always be better writers than those who have had little reading experience. In addition to increasing vocabulary, reading allows children to absorb the structure, cadences and patterns of text. They learn about crafting stories, are exposed to sentences and punctuation and experience proper examples of grammar and spelling being used consistently. Hearing different author voices, styles and genres allows children to find their own voice and feel confident writing in different styles themselves. Children who read widely develop an awareness of formality and tone.

Reading good-quality texts allows them access to examples they can mimic, experiment with and one day make their own.

There is value in reading (and rereading) a favourite author with repeating story patterns, characters and word choice, but it is breadth of reading experiences that really makes the difference. When teachers present a range of authors, genres, styles and text types, pupils store up a bank of ideas for their own writing, allowing their creativity and imagination to grow.

As children become more experienced readers and writers, they begin to read as writers. They think about the author's motivation for writing and relationship with the reader. They spot creative use of language and careful word choices. They wonder about the writing process and the choices the author has made. This awareness can be modelled. As teachers read with pupils, they can pause and take time to question the author's intentions. This doesn't need to be all the time or completely stop the flow of a great story, but at carefully selected moments adults may prompt children to think like the author and look at the text in a new way (Corbett, 2012).

Purpose and audience

Professor Teresa Cremin of the Open University is one of the UK's foremost experts on primary English. She summarises the dilemma faced by teachers like this: teaching writing is 'a balancing act', where children require both knowledge of language and freedom to play with it, and where teachers must negotiate a tension between process and product (Cremin, 2017). Her key argument, though, is that writing becomes meaningful only when children understand the purpose of it, and when they view themselves – and their teachers – as writers with something worth saying.

Whenever adults write, it is for a specific purpose – even if that purpose is for enjoyment, relaxation or reflection. We must provide children with the same opportunities to find purpose in their writing. Often, teachers get stuck making sure children experience a wide range of text types, and end up with dead-end tasks and no real purpose. Instead, they should strive to provide authentic writing experiences with real purpose and real audience. Only then will children find true motivation and intention in their writing.

Purposes for writing include:

- to entertain
- to inform
- to persuade
- to express feelings.

All these purposes are very worthy and have real-life meaning. Children may wish to write a funny story, tell someone about the plight of polar bears as Arctic sea ice recedes, convince someone to stop littering or keep a personal journal that helps them think through their emotions. As children become more mindful about their writing purposes and the audience for their writing, informed choices about text type, structure, use of language, formality and other devices will become easier because they actually have an impact on the finished piece of writing. When children know their audience, their writer's voice becomes stronger. They are able to write with conviction and empathy – more empowered as writers.

It is essential that teachers act on these purposes and actually send children's writing out into the world. It may be a short-story competition, a non-fiction book for younger children, a persuasive letter to their local MP, information leaflets for the community or posters to display around school. When children see their writing having an impact, their self-esteem grows and they want to write more.

In 2024, the Annual Literacy Survey from the National Literacy Trust showed that children writing for enjoyment is at its lowest level since 2010, with only 28.7% of those aged 8–18 doing so (National Literacy Trust, 2024). Teachers must strive to increase the concept of writing for pleasure by showing children how, when and where people enjoy writing: experience of personal journals; writing fiction and letting their imaginations soar; expressing feelings through poetry; writing letters or emails to family and friends; or researching topics of interest and reflecting on what they've discovered.

Ownership, choice and voice

Teaching writing is a fine balance between meeting curriculum objectives and giving children ownership over their writing. When provided with choice, engagement often increases because pupils are writing about something that matters to them. With greater ownership comes greater pride and greater pleasure in writing.

This doesn't mean teachers must relinquish control entirely. There may still be opportunities to let pupils choose the topic, text type, features to include or audience for their writing, depending on the focus of the lesson. Making these decisions together builds a collaborative writing environment and allows pupils truly to own what they create.

Ownership and voice go hand in hand. Children's author Jasmine A. Stirling describes writer's voice as something playful rather than technical: a tool children can pick up, try on and put back down, like a hat or shoes (Stirling, 'How to teach kids about writer's voice'). How we frame voice matters in the classroom. If we treat it as a set quality that children either have or don't, some pupils may feel unable to develop it. When we treat voice as play, every child can try on different voices. Gradually, they will find their voice, and their writing will begin to sound like them.

Writing as a process: an overview

Publishing is not an add-on to the writing process. It is the point at which children experience writing as something to be shared. Sharing writing that is read aloud in assembly, displayed in the corridor or bound into a book for the class library allows children to see themselves as authors: curating their work by deciding what stays and what goes; noticing how their writing lands with a reader; taking pride in something that has left their exercise book and entered the world.

Sadie Phillips is a primary teacher who wrote about her class's self-publishing journey. She describes her experience as an invaluable learning journey, one in which children live out the decisions, challenges and methods that every author goes through (Literacy with Miss P, 2018b).

Authors may joke about being a 'planner' or a 'pantser' (someone who writes 'by the seat of their pants' with little planning), but there is a process common to most writers. This process gives children a clear framework for writing, helping them to move forward, while ensuring they go back to revise and edit along the way. The 'Writing In Action' section later in this chapter works through each stage in turn, with practical strategies for teaching it in the classroom.

Inspiration for writing

Every piece of writing begins with an idea. These ideas may come from life experience, research or some sort of creative stimulus. Teachers risk stunting children's ability to write well if they expect them simply to pluck ideas out of thin air. Many children do not have the adequate background knowledge to pull together the characterisation, setting, possible plot ideas or facts required for a detailed piece of writing. This is why inspiration is essential. It provides children with a bank of ideas to draw on, empowering them in their own writing and creating greater enjoyment in the writing process.

Children's fiction

There are so many high-quality children's books that immerse children in story language, effective structure, author's voice, imaginative characters and detailed settings. Used as a model or prompt for writing, these books give children an idea of how they can use the same techniques in their own writing. This could be a class read aloud that is presented as an example in a writing lesson or a class book that is built into an English unit of shared reading and writing.

Non-fiction

Many recently published non-fiction books are incredibly appealing. In this case, you really can judge a book by its cover. Heavily illustrated, with bright and engaging images, readers are immediately pulled in. Rather than potentially off-putting full pages of text, the information is often broken up into manageable chunks, drawing the reader's eyes around the page. Layout and illustrations work together to aid children's understanding of the whole text. Encouraging children to use these high-quality texts as models for presentation, as well as technical language, sentence construction, text structure and tone, will inspire them to present their facts with authority and creativity.

Videos

The power of a story told on-screen with an emotive soundtrack and meaningful dialogue (or no dialogue at all) captivates children and ignites their imaginations. Using a video as a prompt for writing gives children the opportunity to develop their ability to structure a plot, write speech, enhance characterisation or describe a scene. The Literacy Shed is a website that provides a collection of high-quality videos that are excellent inspiration for writing (www.literacyshed.com). Organised by theme or genre, including 'The Fantasy Shed', 'The Mystery Shed' and 'The Inventors Shed', teachers can find something for every year group across so many topics.

Artefacts and interesting objects

Bringing an unusual object into the classroom is a sure-fire way to pique children's interest. Whether it's a suitcase of mysterious items, a strange rock or a historical artefact, children will have questions. Rich discussion, descriptive vocabulary and making inferences about its origin or use will lead to numerous writing opportunities – for example, a fact file about the object, including the object in a story or a character description of the owner.

Role play

Using drama activities as stimulus allows teachers to design learning experiences that will lead to empathetic writing. Through role play, children may meet characters, become a part of a community, discuss issues, develop a sense of story and understand different perspectives. Whether these experiences are created in school or provided by a theatre company like Alive and Kicking (https://aaktheatre.wordpress.com), they are sure to be memorable and leave children with so many ideas for writing a range of text types.

School trips and visitors

Some of children's most memorable experiences are the trips out of the classroom and special visitors who come into school. Making use of a specialist gives children a fresh perspective, more detailed information and the benefit of expertise. Often, these experiences are quite hands-on and interactive, allowing children to gain a deeper understanding of the topic. Visitors with a personal connection to a topic, such as war, refugees or a food bank, will build empathy and encourage children to write with greater passion.

Writing In Action: instructional strategies

Real purposes for writing

Providing pupils with real purposes for writing is empowering and strengthens their author's voice. Whenever possible, try to find real reasons to write. This may be a letter to the headteacher asking for a rule change or the opportunity to run a fundraising event. It could be an advertisement for a school event or a jingle for a new product created in D&T lessons.

Writing competitions engage and encourage children to create the best possible final draft. The BBC's 500 Words story-writing competition (www.bbc.co.uk/teach/500-words) celebrates writing for pleasure and is a great way to give writers a clear purpose and something to aim for. It is not accurate spelling or the use of different types of punctuation that creates a successful story; it is the creativity, imagination and voice of the writer that counts. With a live-launch lesson to generate ideas, fantastic sample stories from previous winners and tips from top authors, the competition website is a wealth of resources for teachers.

If displaying children's work, make sure it is at eye level and the text is large enough to read. Place value on their words by making sure those looking at the display are able to read and appreciate everything that has gone into the writing.

Laura Buczko from One Education recommends using a RAFT structure to help children write for world-based rather than school-based purposes (Buczko, 2020):

R Reason for writing: What is the authentic purpose for writing?

A Audience: Who is this writing for? How will this impact writing decisions?

F Features: Which features will you include to make your writing effective for your purpose and audience?

T Tone: Persuasive, factual, friendly – how will you get your point across?

Using this structure will help children focus on their desired purpose and intended audience for each piece of writing.

The writing process

Pre-writing and planning strategies

Model how to use pre-writing strategies so pupils are clear about how to tackle them. Speak your thoughts aloud as you wonder about what you're writing, make decisions and add or discard ideas. Encourage pupils to use this as a time to think and discover. They don't have to know everything about what they're going to write. Take time to explore and find new ideas.

Here are some pre-writing strategies to try together:

- Make decisions about audience and purpose now, so the direction of the writing is clear.
- Learn to make notes without copying word for word from a resource.

- Use brainstorming to jot down everything you can think of about an idea. There are no right or wrong answers at this point.
- Make a list of all the points you want to make, then refine and organise them later.
- Use free writing to write down everything you can think of about a topic. This will get the mind flowing and unlock ideas.
- Use questions to prompt ideas – who, what, when, where, why, how?
- Use clustering to gather ideas into categories. This works well following brainstorming, listing or free writing. You may wish to draw circles on your page to cluster your ideas.
- Create a mind-map to show relationships between points.
- Create an outline for writing. Start to think about the structure of your writing. What have you discovered in your pre-writing that will inform the paragraphs you need to write? Keep the outline simple. A graphic organiser may be used as a pre-made outline.
- Use graphic organisers to make sense of your notes and ideas (there are many styles available online). Think about the structure of your writing: the beginning, middle and end; the shape of your narrative; how many paragraphs you might write; or key points for and against in a discussion.

Drafting

Encourage children just to write and get the first draft down on paper. Don't worry too much about spelling and punctuation at this point. As long as the draft can be read by the child, getting ideas down on paper is most important (Rockin Resources, 2014).

Revising and editing will come later. Some schools like to leave space for this by asking children to write on every second line or write only on the left (or right) page, leaving the other page for future drafts. Others use editing margins, where a vertical line is drawn down the page about two-thirds of the way across. This leaves enough space for rewriting sentences or making notes about revisions.

Remind children to use their ideas and notes from the pre-writing stage. Having done this ahead of time should mean they know where to begin and have manageable chunks of writing to tackle.

Be mindful of the amount of time you are asking children to write. Pause and bring them back together as a group to talk about how it's going. Ask them to read back what they've written, to check for sense and that it is following the plan. Going 'rogue' and deviating from their original plan is OK, but encourage them to have a revised plan for where they think their writing is going next.

Watch for pupils who want to write forever. These lengthy pieces can lack focus and never really end. Remind these children to check back on their outline and think about how they will draw their writing to a conclusion.

In contrast, some children find the blank page intimidating. Teachers may offer support by providing smaller pieces of paper, an opening sentence, sentence starters or questions to answer. Sometimes all it takes is getting past the first sentence for the ideas to start to flow.

Modelled writing
Model the drafting process for children. Show them your thinking and emphasise being creative. Allow them to witness the strategies you use while writing, including word choice, sentence construction, what you do if you don't know how to spell a word and rereading the sentence to check you're happy with it. A visualiser and a teacher's writing notebook are valuable resources for this process.

Shared writing
Work together with pupils to create a piece of writing, providing questions and prompts for pupils to make suggestions. Create sentences together in this way.

Guided writing
Work with a small group of pupils, focusing on a specific objective. Through direct teaching, modelling and questioning, guide pupils to produce their own piece of writing.

Revising

Revising writing is changing the ideas themselves. It is not the same as editing, where children correct spelling errors and fix punctuation. Revision is reading the sentences they've created and making changes to improve the content. Encourage pupils to add more descriptive phrases, change the order of sentences for better flow and delete unnecessary detail.

The key focus for revising writing should be the effect on the intended audience. If children know why they are making a change – for example, adding details to create greater suspense in a scary section or increasing the pace through the use of short, punchy sentences – they will become more intentional as writers. Simply relying on a checklist of success criteria will only result in words and phrases being thrown in with no real purpose. This sense of audience and purpose can be taught in the opening sessions of an English unit when pupils are analysing model texts.

Read writing aloud

Reading aloud helps children to hear what sounds right and where sentences do not flow well. It allows them to experience their writing afresh and stops them from skimming through what they think they've written rather than what is actually on the page.

Coloured pens

Many schools develop a routine of using different-coloured pens for revising, so teachers can clearly see where changes have been made. These might be 'purple polishing pens' or 'green fix-it pens'. Using a different colour from the one they originally wrote in makes their revisions stand out. Using different-coloured pens is also helpful when children are revising in pairs. Each child using a different colour means the teacher can tell which are the child's own revisions and which are suggestions from their partner.

Making use of the page

As mentioned in the drafting stage, there are various ways to leave room for revisions and editing. This may be training pupils to write on every second line, writing on one page and leaving the other blank or using revising margins. Consistency across school will really help this become a habit and make revision time more meaningful. Revision will be messy, but it is an important part of the process.

Some teachers use writing flaps. This is where another small piece of paper is taped along one edge, over the top of the original paragraph. Children rewrite their sentence or paragraph on the flap as a second draft. Tracing paper also works well to encourage children to write new sentences over the top of their existing writing.

DARE to revise

Rockin Resources challenges children to DARE to revise their writing (Rockin Resources, 2015):

D Delete unnecessary information.

A Add more important detail and transition words.

R Rearrange text to be logical and effective.

E Exchange words for clearer or stronger ones.

The 'boxed' or 'expanding' success criteria
Rather than using generic lists of success criteria to encourage revision, English adviser James Durran has created a planning and revision tool that encourages pupils really to focus on the purpose of their writing and develop 'success criteria' from there. For example, in a scary story, writers will want their readers actually to feel scared; they know they can achieve this through spooky similes and frightening nouns. In an information leaflet about pet ownership for children, writers may want to persuade their readers to look after their animals properly; they can achieve this through command verbs and rhetorical questions.

For guidance on how to use this strategy, visit Durran (2019).

Revising in pairs
Working together can allow children to speak more freely about their writing and share ideas. Always give them the opportunity to read through and make some revisions on their own first. This will help the revision process with a partner run much more smoothly.

When introducing a peer revising lesson, it's important pupils understand the purpose and audience of their partner's writing. By focusing on these elements, they can suggest more meaningful changes (rather than just 'You missed a capital letter') and the children can really get to grips with more powerful writing.

Using a different-coloured pen is one way for partners to make suggestions, but some children dislike having anyone else write on their work. Using sticky notes to add suggestions leaves the writer with full control over their draft.

See 'Further reading' for a Teachwire article in which Shirley Clarke shares strategies for peer revision and editing.

Motivation to revise
Some children are very precious about what they've written and don't want to spoil their first drafts. Using tracing paper or a writing flap can help to take away this anxiety, while still encouraging them to make improvements.

Model making meaningful revisions by sharing the writing process of real-life authors. What do their first drafts look like? How do they make revisions? How long did it take them to write their book? Realising that every great writer makes changes to their writing, and that writing isn't 'finished' after just one draft, is a powerful message for children to understand.

Author S.F. Said shared the 17 drafts of his 2003 book *Varjak Paw* in an article for the British Library. He has reproduced this content on his own website (Said, 2024). It is a wonderful example of how first drafts change and how investing time in a piece of writing can make such a difference. Children aren't going to spend five years on a piece of writing, but this example shows them that even the best writers have to work at their craft.

Editing

Editing writing can be a very vague task for pupils in primary school. When asked to 'check their work', they give it a glance but can often miss many errors. As with every other stage, this point in the writing process needs to be explicitly modelled and taught, so that children are effective in their editing, make real changes to their writing and develop independent editing skills. To edit successfully, children must learn to manage a number of different skills involving spelling, punctuation and grammar.

The first step is discussing how mistakes aren't failures to conceal but the foundation of better writing. Everybody edits, including all the authors children love. S.F. Said, the aforementioned writer of *Varjak Paw* and *Phoenix* (2013) is refreshingly open about his editing process: it took 13 drafts for *Phoenix* to become the book he wanted to read and, as with *Varjak Paw*, he has published an early draft alongside the final copy so readers can compare them (Said, 2017). His guidance to other writers could hardly be simpler: become a reader. Once a draft exists, Said argues, the writer must stand back and ask of their own work the questions they would ask of any story. What's working? What's not? What can be expanded? What can be cut? Then they return to the page, and keep returning, until the story is as good as they can make it.

This is a powerful frame for children. If a published author isn't afraid to write 13, or even 17, drafts, the idea that their own work might need two or three versions starts to feel reasonable rather than punitive. Where possible, connect this practice to the writers children admire: an in-person or online author visit is a chance to ask these questions of working writers, and children tend to remember what an author says about revision far longer than any single lesson on the subject.

Editing stations

Using editing stations guides pupils to focus on one area at a time. Each station can be tailored to the needs of the class, allowing them to address learning targets and common errors identified while children are drafting, or in previous pieces of writing.

Create a number of stations around the classroom resourced with model sentences demonstrating the objective, posters explaining the rule, dictionaries, word banks, pens, highlighters and anything else that will support the editing. Teachers should model what is expected at each station.

Independently, in pairs or in groups, pupils should visit each station in turn. While there, they focus only on making changes to their writing linked to the objective of the station. This could be adding capital letters to proper nouns, checking for the use of a comma after an opening subordinate clause or identifying spellings they are unsure of and checking them in a dictionary or word bank. Once children have visited each station, they will have made significant edits in their writing.

Practising editing

Sometimes children can be quite blind to errors in their own writing. They are so invested in a piece (or have spent so much time on it already) that they want it to be finished. Teaching them to edit writing that is not their own will allow them to gain some distance from the writing and really focus on changes that need to be made. Spotting someone else's errors is fun.

Give children a piece of writing containing errors similar to those they tend to make as a class. Practise making edits together, in pairs and then independently as their skill and confidence grows.

Alan Peat Sentences

Alan Peat is an educational consultant and writer. He has written many books aimed at encouraging children to write creatively, including *Writing Exciting Sentences* (2008). His sentence types provide teachers with a framework for teaching children to write grammatically correct sentences with variety and flare. The sentence structures provided are high-quality models for children to emulate in building their own sentences. From simple sentences to those involving multiple clauses and advanced punctuation, using Alan Peat's sentence types as a whole-school initiative provides a common language in describing sentence structure, and clear progression. This framework is unique in how it embeds grammar into relevant and accessible strategies pupils can implement and remember.

Examples of Alan Peat sentence types

Challenge pupils to use a 2A sentence (two adjectives before a noun):

'The fierce, ginger cat froze as the timid, grey mouse scurried across the floor.'

Or a De:De sentence in which they learn to use a colon correctly to separate description and details:

'The lion truly is the king of the beasts: its golden mane gives the appearance of royalty.

Publishing

Not every piece of work needs to go through the full writing process, but when time is taken to improve children's writing, it is important they are given the opportunity to create a final draft to be proud of. Children should know the purpose of this final product, whether it's written up for a portfolio or display, to share with another class or to send out into the world.

These final pieces may be handwritten or typed. Putting pen (or pencil) to paper allows children to take pride in their own handwriting, and emphasises the importance of a neat, consistent script. Handwritten pieces are also likely to be completed more quickly and with fewer transcription errors. However, in this technical age, the ability to use a computer and type efficiently is essential. Publishing finished writing on a computer gives the work a more 'professional' feel and allows it to be shared electronically or printed out for a class book or display.

Text types

Text types are a method of categorising pieces of writing by purpose and structure. In primary school, pupils may write to recount an event, inform, instruct, explain, persuade or discuss. They may write to entertain or tell a story. Within each of these purposes, there are different text types children learn to help organise their ideas in a coherent manner. Not all writing fits into just one text type so, as children develop as writers, they are able to combine writing purposes and create texts containing features of multiple types. For example, they may write a persuasive letter or a newspaper article in which they discuss both sides of an issue.

Narrative writing

Narrative writing is categorised by genre – for example, contemporary, traditional, fantasy, comedy, horror, mystery, historical, science fiction, adventure. Writers often combine genres to create engaging, unique stories. Having an understanding of the typical features of each genre helps children to express themselves while developing style and voice.

Non-fiction writing

Non-fiction writing is categorised by purpose: to recount, inform, instruct, explain, persuade or discuss. Within each of these purposes, there are a number of different text types:

Table 3.2 Non-fiction purposes

Recount	Inform	Instruct
• letter • diary • journal • 'captain's log'	• report • news article • biography • autobiography	• recipe • game instructions • science investigations • assembly instructions
Explain	**Persuade**	**Discuss**
• natural phenomena • scientific processes	• advertisements • jingles • leaflets • letter	• balanced argument • debate

In his Teachwire article 'Let's not abandon text types', James Clements discusses the move away from focusing on text types with the 2014 curriculum and how a balanced approach to the teaching of writing provides opportunities for creativity and the use of text types to encourage children to write for purpose. He encourages teachers and children to have fun with text types by combining them in interesting ways: 'As children grow older, the writing they produce won't fit neatly into one of the primary school text types. If we want a generation of children who can use language with confidence, selecting words and phrases to communicate their ideas clearly and powerfully, then we need to teach them to be flexible in their writing' (Clements, a).

In 2013, the National Literacy Trust created a very useful guide to text types (National Literacy Trust, 2013). This document provides details about structural and language features for each text type, as well as strategies for the writer.

Skeleton frames

There is a common language when describing the conventions of different text types. For example, recounts are usually written in chronological order, while instructions use imperative verbs to tell the reader what to do. Pupils must become familiar with these structural and language features to write effectively in their desired format. This does not need to become a tick list of dry elements, but rather tools to use as they write for a particular purpose. Most writing does not fit neatly into one specific text type, but having an awareness of a variety of structures will help children organise their ideas in a coherent manner.

Literacy specialist Sue Palmer created a series of skeleton frame books for structuring non-fiction text types. Originally produced as big books (such as *The Discussion Book* and *The Report Book*), these skeleton frames give children a clear picture of how to structure each type of writing. Perfect for teaching the structure of a text type and for the planning stage of the writing process, many children find these frames helpful for visualising the path their writing will take (Palmer, 2006; Palmer and Corbett, 2003).

Using these writing skeletons across school provides pupils with that common language and allows them to build up their repertoire of writing text types over time.

See 'Further reading' for details of how to watch Sue Palmer's 2016 video 'Skeletons for Organising Writing'.

Blocks of genres versus multiple genre units

Within the Primary Literacy Strategy and Primary Framework for Literacy (preceding the national curriculum in 2014), writing units were largely focused on a specific text type. This led to tick lists of success criteria and little cohesion between units, as many features were specific to just one text type. Pupils spent a short amount of time learning one set of techniques before moving on to another. The result was often insecure learning and the need to revise techniques each time a text type was revisited (often a year later).

Over the last number of years, many educators have looked at ways to combine text types into more cohesive units focusing on writing with intent. Rather than emphasising the features of each text type, more central skills at word, sentence and text level, such as powerful word choice, the use of conjunctions or developing paragraphs, have taken priority across multiple text types. Michael Tidd discusses this strategy in his blog posts, 'Why is mastery just for maths?' (October 2013), 'A mastery model for writing: moving away from the text type treadmill' (June 2014) and 'Writing for a purpose (or 4!)' (August 2016). Focusing on writing to entertain, inform, persuade and discuss, he groups text types to allow children opportunities to develop the same skills in different pieces of writing. This strategy gets to the heart of good-quality writing and makes steps towards avoiding formulaic writing that only follows the success criteria. Children come to understand that each text type is not used for just one purpose. For example, a letter may inform, persuade or show feelings.

Another approach is to use the shared class book as the driver for writing opportunities. This must be carefully planned to ensure a range of writing experiences across the year and so the class's learning is in line with the school's overall plan for writing. One book may inspire a whole host of text types and genres. In this case, the purpose for writing really does take centre stage. Children may write a letter to a character, an additional chapter to explore another point of view, a diary through the voice of the main character or a newspaper article of an event in the story. These writing choices may be directed by the teacher or selected by the children.

From our own reading experiences, we know that not every piece of writing slots neatly into one specific text type or genre. Similarly, each text type is not used for just one purpose. We come across recipes that provide background information about ingredients or cooking techniques, science fiction fantasy and historical mystery. Allowing children to experiment with combining text types or choosing the text type that best meets the needs of their purposes provides more meaningful writing and unleashes creativity.

Visit the website of the CLPE (Centre for Literacy in Primary Education) to see 'Writing in Primary Schools: What We Know Works', which has 10 solid ideas for teaching writing (see 'Further reading').

Spelling: instructional strategies

See Chapter 5 to read about the debates around spelling tests.

When it comes to spelling instruction, there is so much more than 'read, cover, write, check' and practising for spelling tests. By the time they leave primary school, competent spellers are using four main strategies to learn and remember words (Rippel, 2009).

Spelling instruction should be a balance of explicit, direct teaching and integrated learning during reading and writing sessions. Make it a habit to notice spellings you've been learning as a class, and give pupils lots of opportunities to self-check and apply their spelling knowledge.

Phonetic strategies

First introduced in Early Years and key stage 1, phonetic spelling involves spelling words as we hear them – using the sounds of letters to work out the spelling. By segmenting (or breaking down) words into their sounds, children can assign the correct letters as they write. This strategy builds confidence in pupils, as they are able to use many of the correct letters and devise plausible spellings.

Rule-based strategies

Rule-based spelling strategies come into play when the spelling of a word does not follow phonetics. Teachers need to explain the rules to pupils and give them time to practise and apply their knowledge. Displaying spelling rules and revisiting them often will help pupils internalise them.

It is important that teachers have a strong understanding of the reasons behind the rules, so they are able to explain them clearly to pupils. Using a quality spelling scheme will help teachers develop their own word knowledge as they teach.

Visual strategies

Using visual strategies for spelling is key when words are irregular. These 'sight words' require a whole-word strategy. Once children can accurately visualise the word, they'll be able to spell it every time.

The best way to build visual memory of words is through reading and being read to. Word games and word walls also help with being able to picture words and know whether they look 'right'. Visual strategies are particularly important for learning homophones.

Morphemic strategies

Using morphemic spelling strategies involves understanding the meaning of words as well as the spelling. By applying knowledge of root words, prefixes and suffixes, pupils can build words based on meaning and related words they already know.

Self-checking

In addition to these strategies, teaching children to self-check their spelling is key to creating competent, confident spellers.

There will always be words we don't know how to spell. Knowing how to find out empowers children and puts a whole world of words at their fingertips.

Teach pupils to use print and online dictionaries to check their spelling and to:

- develop confidence with alphabetical order
- use the guide letters at the top of the page
- identify the first two or three letters of the word
- think of alternative spellings if their first guess doesn't find it (e.g. *ph* instead of *f*)
- search for related words or a definition on the internet
- spell a word phonetically and take note of spellcheck or autocorrect.

Methods for learning spellings

Rhyming

Rhymes show children how common sounds can turn into common spellings. Start by playing with words orally, then begin to create lists of rhyming words (hot – not – pot – shot). Children can experiment with how many words they can create from a simple starting word.

Chunking

Break words into chunks for easier spelling. For example, 'jumping' can be broken down into [j] [ump] [ing]. Children will start to recognise familiar patterns and apply them to other words.

Words within words

Spotting smaller words within larger words will help children remember their spelling. Can they find 'table' within 'vegetable' or 'end' within 'friend'?

Chaining

Build up words one letter at a time. Start by looking at and copying the whole word. Say each letter as you write it. Then rewrite the word again underneath, adding one letter each time. For example:

star
s
st
sta
star

▲ **Figure 3.1 Chaining**

Pyramid writing

Use the chaining method to create a word pyramid. For example:

p
py
pyr
pyra
pyram
pyrami
pyramid

▲ **Figure 3.2 Pyramid writing**

Reverse chaining by letter or syllable

Use the chaining method again but, this time, drop one letter (or syllable) off the end of the word each time you write it. Say each letter (including the missing ones) as you write. For example:

frame	ex-press-ive
fram_	ex-press-___
fra__	ex-_____-___
fr___	__-_____-___
f____	
_____	

▲ **Figure 3.3 Reverse chaining by letter or syllable**

Highlighting the hard parts

Write the word and think about which bit causes trouble. Highlight those letters and think about the pattern or rule. Write the word again with the hard part in a different colour or so it stands out in some way. Whenever you write the word, think about that tricky bit.

Fill in the missing letters

Practise spelling words with similar sounds by filling in missing letters. Give children a bank of letter strings to choose from. For example:

Choose from tion / sion / cean:

o____

direc____

televi____

▲ **Figure 3.4 Fill in the missing letters**

Tracing words

Tracing words helps children visualise spellings and develops muscle memory. It can be done in lots of ways, from something as simple as writing a word on a piece of paper and going over it with a pencil or finger, to writing letters in sand, foam or paint over laminated sheets.

Speed writing

Choose a word. How many times can it be written accurately in 30 seconds or one minute? Repeated correct spelling helps children to visualise the word and builds muscle memory.

Word shapes

Being able to visualise the shape of the letters that make up a word is key for picturing what the word looks like on the page. Draw boxes around each letter to determine whether it is tall, has a descender, or is a small letter that sits on the line. When pupils are given the empty boxes, can they choose the correct word from a word bank and fill it in correctly? For example:

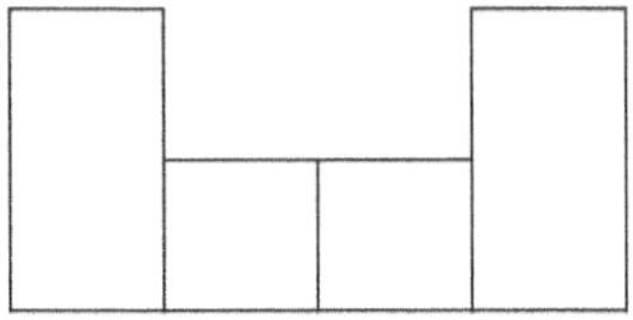

= look

▲ **Figure 3.5 Word shape for 'look'**

Spot the odd one out

Knowing when a spelling looks wrong is key for teaching children to self-check and help their peers to edit their writing. Give pupils a list of words in which just one word is spelled incorrectly. Can they spot it? Do they know how to correct it? For example:

accommodate	acompany	according

▲ **Figure 3.6 Spot the odd one out**

Mnemonics

Using memory aids can help children remember specific words or spelling rules.

necessary – a shirt has one collar and two sleeves (one c and two s)

pieces – pieces of a pie

▲ **Figure 3.7 Mnemonics**

Building sentences

During the drafting and revising stage of the writing process, children require sentence-building and editing tools. Frameworks providing this support have become popular in primary practice; Alan Peat's sentence types (see the section titled 'Alan Peat Sentences' earlier in this chapter) are some of the most widely used, as they provide teachers and children with common language for talking about sentence construction, as well as a clear idea of progression throughout a school.

Further reading

Clarke, S. '5 steps for better peer marking'. Teachwire, www.teachwire.net/news/shirley-clarkes-five-steps-to-better-peer-marking-in-the-primary-classroom/

Clements, J., 'Let's not abandon text types: used creatively they can still support children'. Teachwire, www.teachwire.net/news/lets-not-abandon-text-types-used-creatively-they-can-still-support-children/

CLPE, 'Writing in Primary Schools: What We Know Works', https://clpe.org.uk/research/writing-primary-schools-what-we-know-works

Durran, J. (2019) 'Re-thinking "success criteria": a simple device to support pupils' writing', https://jamesdurran.blog/2019/01/24/re-thinking-success-criteria-a-simple-device-to-support-pupils-writing/

Palmer, S. (2016) 'Skeletons for Organising Writing' [video], www.youtube.com/watch?v=PGkKEq3QnJM

Tidd, M. (2013, 2014, 2016) 'A Mastery Model for Writing' [three blog posts]: https://michaelt1979.wordpress.com/2013/10/18/why-is-mastery-just-for-maths/, https://michaelt1979.wordpress.com/2014/06/30/a-mastery-model-for-writing-moving-away-from-the-text-type-treadmill/, https://michaelt1979.wordpress.com/2016/08/29/writing-for-a-purpose-or-4/

CHAPTER 4
MODE B: NON-INSTRUCTIONAL STRATEGIES

We sometimes fall into the trap of thinking that English teaching is what happens 'in the English lesson'. This chapter shows otherwise. A lot of what makes us think 'this feels like a reading classroom' or 'this feels like a writing classroom', for example, isn't actually taught at all: it's in the ethos of the room. The posters on the walls, the routines that have been developed, the language you hear as you walk into the room and the decisions that teachers make about what they will model and what they will let pupils discover for themselves. This should run alongside the direct teaching explored in Chapters 1–3; when it works well, these explicit and implicit teaching techniques complement each other.

In his book, *The Learning Rainforest: Great Teaching in Real Classrooms* (2017), Tom Sherrington introduces the concept of Mode A and Mode B teaching. Mode A is the typical teacher-led instruction that makes up most primary English lessons. Mode B teaching is a wider collection of activities in which pupils are given opportunities to make choices, work collaboratively and spend more time talking about their learning. These are not necessarily stand-alone activities. They can be woven into a unit of work to give pupils a fuller learning experience.

Collaborative learning

Working in groups can be an effective classroom technique. Pupils are able to share points of view, divide up the workload and discuss new learning. One of the greatest benefits of group work is the opportunity for talk. Children are able to mix with others in the class while the teacher circulates, adding to discussions and monitoring the speaking and listening going on. During these activities, pupils are able to develop leadership and learn to follow the lead of their peers. They must take more responsibility for their learning and find success as they achieve together (Hayes, 2020).

However, for group work to have an impact, pupils need to learn how to work together and stay focused on the task at hand. Take time to establish rules and routines so everyone knows what is expected. Not everyone can speak at once, so set up roles – perhaps one child will talk, the second will listen and the third will take notes.

Enquiry projects

An enquiry project is an excellent way to combine speaking, listening, reading and writing skills in one extended task. It also allows children to make meaningful connections with other areas of the curriculum, such as science, geography and history.

Once children have learned sufficient knowledge in their area of study, they can be prompted to think of questions that will extend their learning. As they find answers to these questions, they may draw conclusions or come up with even more questions.

An example of an extended enquiry project is the Spring Chicken Project in Year 1 at Farsley Farfield Primary School in Leeds. Children work in groups to find out more about the chickens who live on their school farm. They ask questions of the headteacher, groundskeeper and others who care for the chickens, spend time reading and watching videos for more information and then present their findings in their own chicken books (non-chronological reports). They also work together to create short animated videos. The books and videos are shared with parents at a special Spring Chicken event, complete with a rousing rendition of the song 'I'm a Spring Chicken'.

> The children always enjoy the chicken project and it is a highlight of their time in Year 1. They like to interview our headteacher and find out lots of interesting chicken facts. They spend time writing and illustrating their own chicken non-fiction book. The children are always very proud of their finished book and are keen to share it with their families.
>
> **Alex Galbraith, teacher at Farsley Farfield Primary School**

Debate

Debate is a key technique for developing structure and conviction in spoken language. As children express their views, listen to others and respond respectfully, their understanding deepens, and they develop confidence and assertiveness. They become better able to recognise opposing viewpoints, and learn how to speak persuasively and react to challenge.

Units of work based around issues and dilemmas are the perfect home for debate. Whether it's discussing environmental issues read in non-fiction texts, considering choices faced by young people in magazine articles or analysing the actions of characters in fiction and poetry, giving children the opportunity to formulate arguments and present their side of the debate can be powerful.

'The Highwayman' is a popular classic poem in upper key stage 2. Children are fascinated by the secret relationship between Bess and the Highwayman, Tim the ostler lurking in the shadows and the despicable actions of King George's men. A courtroom trial (debate) about who was ultimately to blame for Bess's death brings all the issues of the narrative poem to the fore, prompting children to think deeply about the language as well as the cause and effect of the characters' actions. They are challenged to make inferences about how each character was feeling and how those feelings influenced their actions. When given the opportunity to take on the role of Bess's father and follow up by writing a letter to the judge about who they believe is to blame, children write passionately, with detailed reasons to back up their views.

Open response tasks

Once children come to the end of a unit of work exploring a theme, genre or text, and have acquired a great deal of knowledge, it's the perfect time to present the challenge of an open response task. They may shape their response to the task in any way they choose: an essay, a poster, a poem, a song, a diorama, a model, a painting, a short play – anything that expresses their learning. The richness of responses will allow everyone to think about the topic in a new way.

Many secondary schools provide their key stage 3 pupils with valuable opportunities to share their knowledge of English topics through open response tasks. These types of activities can also be very successful in key stage 2. At Abbey Grange Church of England Academy, children are challenged to respond to a statement about something they've been studying (e.g. 'Young characters are presented negatively in Shakespeare plays' or 'Futuristic and dystopian literature is always bleak in its outlook'). Encouraged to debate, they work in groups or individually to create a project that reflects their view of the statement. After a number of weeks, the final projects are showcased.

Our aims with this programme, beyond promoting independent learning and a love of literature, are to provide cultural capital, promote critical thinking and deeper questioning of texts. The tasks are all aimed to make the pupils consider writers' aims and intentions more critically and in a conceptual way, moving beyond obvious interpretations to confidently form their own opinions. All tasks ask them to engage in a debate.

Students love being with like-minded students and having the option to work in any medium they choose. The more creative the better, we say. We have had various amazing projects from pieces of music to mood boards, artwork, cakes, films, interviews with actors, and poetry. Staff love being part of the celebration and the work we get is incredible.

Micaela Romero, KS3 English teacher at Abbey Grange Church of England Academy

Recitation and performance

Poetry competition or poetry slam

An oral poetry competition is a fantastic opportunity to encourage children to listen to, learn and memorise a selection of high-quality poems. Whether it's classics, modern or even a genuine poetry slam where children write their own poetry around a specific theme, learning poems to perform 'by heart' allows children to play with words while focusing on their sounds and meaning. The musicality of poetry builds a sense of rhythm. The layers of meaning in poetry develop emotional intelligence. Children are able to drill down into the real purposes of the poems they're performing and experiment with communicating that meaning to others.

The Reading Agency gives advice about how to run a poetry slam in your own school:

> A slam is the competitive art of performance poetry. Participants (single performers or groups) perform their original work and are judged by members of the audience. Typically, the host selects the judges, who are instructed to give numerical scores (between 0 and 10) based on the poet's content and performance. The audience's job is to keep the mood supportive, energetic and encouraging to all participants.
>
> **The Reading Agency, 'Running a poetry slam'**

If you prefer, run your poetry competition by asking the children to learn a published poem by heart. Learning to interpret someone else's words is such an important skill. Try the Poetry by Heart 'Timeline Anthology' for a wonderful collection of poems and poets (see 'Further reading').

Visit the CLPE (Centre for Literacy in Primary Education) to see Poetry in 'Primary Schools: What We Know Works', which has 10 fantastic ideas for teaching poetry (again, see 'Further reading').

Connecting with authors

Engaging with current and active children's authors and illustrators is a powerful way to promote reading for pleasure in your school. It allows children to interact with positive literary role models, and inspires both reading and writing skills. As detailed in Chapter 2, there are some easy ways to make contact and bring authors into your classroom.

Class trips

Learning outside the classroom is a powerful way for pupils to gain new vocabulary and life experiences, consolidate prior knowledge and learn something new. Class trips are sometimes not as obvious when it comes to English but, with some thought and creativity, there are many meaningful, exciting and memorable experiences to be had.

Theatre trips

A visit to see a play or musical is one of the most obvious choices for taking English outside the classroom. Keep an eye out for flyers or check the websites of your local theatres to see whether anything appropriate comes along. Watch for stories or authors you've read together, or plays with similar themes. Some children's books are now being adapted for the stage with wonderful results. Sophie Anderson's *The House with Chicken Legs* is just one example of an incredible middle-grade novel being turned into a play. Picture books are also finding their way to the stage. Lu Fraser and Kate Hindley's *The Littlest Yak* is being shared with young audiences through adorable puppetry.

Theatre workshops are also often available to give children the opportunity to learn about storytelling and play scripts through first-hand experience.

Activities linked to stories

Think about the theme of your class novel and useful background knowledge that would help a pupil really get into the text.

After teaching Michael Morpurgo's *Kensuke's Kingdom* for a few years, I was preparing for a class with a higher number of children with English as an additional language, as well as children with other communication challenges and limited life experiences. I decided to take my class to the local sailing club as part of our English unit for the half term. I shared my aims with the sailing instructors ahead of time, and they were more than happy to help develop vocabulary and experience of sailing for the children. They read the book before our visit, then chatted with the children about the characters' experiences while they were out sailing.

Visit my website (Heap, 2019) if you'd like to find out more about our sailing experiences.

Historic author homes and museums

If you are lucky enough to live near the historic home of a well-known author, or a museum dedicated to their life, take the opportunity to visit with your class. Often there are engaging children's programmes and opportunities to link your visit to what you've been reading in school. Visit the Roald Dahl Museum and Story Centre in Great Missenden in Buckinghamshire or explore The World of Beatrix Potter at Bowness-on-Windermere.

Special days

The calendar is full of special days linked to English. Use the National Literacy Trust's 'Literacy teaching and school events calendar' to plan your literacy year (https://literacytrust.org.uk/resources/literacy-teaching-calendar). These literary and cultural events will build reading, writing and spoken language skills, and develop cultural awareness and wonderful shared experiences.

Here are a few examples of some special days to mark across the year:

World Book Day

Perhaps the most popular annual event is World Book Day. Celebrated in early March in the UK, its aim is to promote reading for pleasure and allow each child the opportunity to receive a book of their own. It is a fantastic opportunity for schools to engage with authors, highlight new books or explore themed activities across your school. See www.worldbookday.com

National Storytelling Week

Held at the end of January, this week celebrates storytelling and oral tradition. Whether old or modern, stories are meant to be shared. Children are given opportunities to listen to a wide range of stories, and to develop their own storytelling skills. See https://literacytrust.org.uk/resources/national-storytelling-week

Empathy Day

On the Empathy Day page of its website, EmpathyLab describes the vision for this festival as follows: 'Empathy Day celebrates and grows empathy's power to create a better world. It shines a light on books' role in raising an empathy-educated generation. Empathy Day inspires children to learn more about empathy, have transformational experiences through stories, and to put empathy into action!'

Join in with your class in early June and share empathy-rich books from its Read for Empathy collections all year round. See https://empathylab.uk/empathy-day/

National Writing Day

Celebrate writing for enjoyment with National Writing Day in June. Go beyond set tasks and help children explore their creativity. Find new purposes and pleasure in writing. See https://literacytrust.org.uk/about-us/national-writing-day/

Further reading

CLPE, 'Poetry in Primary Schools: What We Know Works', https://clpe.org.uk/research/poetry-primary-schools-what-we-know-works

Heap, K. (2019) 'Learning Beyond the Classroom with Literacy Inspired Outdoor Education'. Scope for Imagination, https://scopeforimagination.co.uk/2019/11/28/learning-beyond-the-classroom-with-literacy-inspired-outdoor-education

Poetry by Heart 'Timeline Anthology', e.g. www.poetrybyheart.org.uk/timeline/7plus

Sherrington, T. and Caviglioli, O. (2020) *Teaching Walkthrus*. John Catt Educational (collaborative learning, p.134; enquiry projects, p.138; oracy – debating, p.142; open response tasks, p.140)

CHAPTER 5
DEBATES AND PERSPECTIVES

Nothing about teaching English is set in stone. Research uncovers new strategies worth trying, old favourites fall in and out of fashion and the ideas we were once told were 'best practice' are challenged. As teachers, we have to keep on top of the latest thinking (Chapter 6 looks at subject-specific research), but it's also important not to ditch long-standing strategies if they're still working well.

Healthy debate is a good thing. Weighing arguments, listening to differing opinions, working out how to articulate our own position – it all helps us refine our practice. In this chapter, I want to address three debates that crop up time and again both in staffrooms and on social media: whole-class reading versus group guided reading; how we reward and manage home reading; and traditional spelling tests. For each one, I'll do my best to represent the pros and cons fairly as I see them, then explain where I stand on each issue and why.

You may not agree with my stance on each of these – and that's absolutely fine. My aim isn't to close down these debates once and for all, but I do hope that by working through each one in detail you'll be able to think it through for yourself and make an informed decision.

Whole-class versus group guided reading

Whole-class reading happens when all pupils in the class take part in a reading lesson together, with a common shared text – on the interactive whiteboard, on copied sheets or through multiple copies of the actual book. The teacher leads the lesson, focusing on vocabulary, pausing to discuss character, plot and the author's use of language and challenging pupils to make inferences. There may be oral discussion of key questions or a written element to the session.

A more traditional approach to teaching reading, group guided reading, is often a carousel of reading activities that take place over the course of a week. The class is split into groups (sometimes by ability) with each group having the opportunity to work with the teacher (or another adult) for at least one session each week. Often, groups read differentiated texts based on their reading ability. On days when a group is not working with an adult, children may be completing follow-up questions, pre-reading for the next session, reading a related text or doing another reading task.

The benefits of whole-class reading

A whole-class reading model ensures all pupils receive input from the expert teacher during every reading lesson. They are not left on their own or, in some cases, always left to work with another adult who may not have the training to provide as high-quality sessions as the teacher.

Teachers are able to provide more intensive reading sessions that link together, each lesson building on the previous one. All pupils are given access to ambitious, age-appropriate texts, and a robust, thoughtful discussion led by an enthusiastic teacher.

Time is used efficiently and a lot more reading teaching happens across the week. It can be argued that whole-class reading is less complicated than group guided reading, as teachers are required to know only one text at a time. They have more time to read, analyse, prepare questions and decide which aspects of the text to delve into more deeply with children.

In whole-class reading lessons, teachers are able to model reading with fluency for all pupils at the same time and more often than in a group scenario. The more children are read to, the sooner they will develop fluency in their own reading.

Concerns about whole-class reading

Some teachers are concerned about moving to the whole-class reading model and have questions:

- If the text choices are ambitious, how will less able readers access them? Wouldn't they be better reading a text at their reading level?
- If the teacher needs to spend time supporting the less able readers, won't the more confident readers be held back and become bored?
- Isn't there more potential to engage all readers in small-group discussions rather than in one large whole-class discussion?

Opportunities for adaptive teaching or differentiating texts and tasks is often the largest concern raised whenever whole-class reading is mentioned. With careful planning and an awareness of each pupil's reading needs, a range of reading abilities can be managed effectively. Consider the following strategies, including some from KS1 expert Gemma Spence (Spence, 2021).

- **Choose the text carefully:** Look for books with potential for depth of discussion. Consider the visual and verbal language of pictures and words. Choose books that are appealing and will engage readers across attainment levels. Aim for books the majority of children can read with 90–94% accuracy (instructional level). Use strategies to help lower-attaining readers prepare for whole-class sessions.
- **Teach the context of the book:** Make links to other areas of learning. Watch videos or read other background materials to set the scene. Discuss the author and time period in which the text was written.
- **Pre-teach vocabulary:** Look carefully at the vocabulary in the text. Choose words that will hamper a general understanding of the text or are not easily defined through context. You don't need to pre-teach every unfamiliar word, but investigating some ahead of reading will allow more children to access the text successfully. It may be that just a select group of children would benefit from this pre-teaching or it may be appropriate for the entire class.
- **Prior reading:** Reading the text ahead of the reading lesson can be incredibly beneficial for children who are still learning to decode fluently. Listening to an adult read the text aloud, reading in groups or reading at their own pace with support will build confidence and allow children to develop their comprehension abilities beyond their independent reading ability.
- **Visual images:** Use images to help children visualise what they are reading. This may be by providing illustrations to accompany the text or asking children to draw their own pictures of what they have read. The use of props such as clothing, small items named in the text or larger items such as an old broomstick or treasure chest will make the learning more memorable.
- **Reading to and with children:** Keep reading lessons engaging and build fluency by using a range of reading strategies. Choral reading, paired reading, individual reading and echo reading are all methods that give children the opportunity to read and engage with the text. A mixed approach allows the teacher to model expressive, fluent reading, while building the same skills in children.
- **Independent activities:** During whole-class reading lessons, there will be times when children are asked to complete a task independently. This is when more traditional differentiation or adaptive strategies could come into play. Children may be asked to complete the same task with varying degrees of support and scaffolding, or they may be

given different tasks. Confident readers may be given opportunities for extension and more challenging analysis, while another group might work with an adult to discuss the importance of a particular character.

- **Model learning with thinking out loud:** Modelling is a key part of teaching whole-class reading lessons. As teachers read a text, they pause and speak aloud their thoughts: questions, predictions, 'aha' moments and links to other texts or everyday life. By encouraging children to do the same, they will become more active readers and be more aware of their thoughts while reading.
- **Use sentence stems for developing answers:** Help children to frame their answers to questions during reading lessons by providing scaffolding through sentence stems such as 'I know the character felt _________ because...' or 'I predict __________ because...' Once confident with oral answers, these sentence stems can then be transferred to written answers.
- **Partner talk:** A valuable strategy in any lesson, partner talk gives everyone a chance to answer a question before contributing to the whole-class discussion. Children have the opportunity to hear what someone else thinks and refine their own answer.
- **Read through twice:** The first time the children read a text, focus on fluency. Use read aloud, choral reading or echo reading to allow them to hear expression and read the entire text beginning to end without stopping. Then, read the text again, this time focusing on comprehension. Pause and model thinking as you read. You may also want to ask questions at key points.
- **Multiple days on the same text:** Use the same extract over a number of days, even for the entire week. Each time you read it, children will become more fluent and develop greater understanding. You may wish to focus on a particular aspect of the text each day and practise a variety of question types. Be conscious of keeping the reading fresh and engaging, so children do not lose interest in the text.

The benefits of group guided reading

Group guided reading provides valuable opportunities for high-quality discussion about books between the teacher and other pupils. The back and forth of this discussion can challenge children to extend their ideas, find evidence to back up their inferences and think more critically about the text. Children are able to ask questions and take risks in their answers, without the pressure of everyone listening.

Children must be taught to find meaning in the text by carefully considering word choices and understanding the nuances of literature. This is not always straightforward. Working in a small group with a teacher allows pupils to explore words and sentences they do not understand. Teachers are able to respond to the needs of the group and provide much more bespoke instruction. Gaps in vocabulary knowledge, queries about grammar and misunderstandings can be addressed quickly, allowing the child to move forwards in their overall understanding of the text.

During whole-class reading sessions, it can be difficult for the teacher to grasp exactly how much of the text and learning objective each child is understanding. The discussion may be buzzing but how can the teacher be sure the lower prior attaining readers are accessing the learning and making good progress? Group guided reading allows teachers to gauge each child's understanding more clearly and hear first-hand the links they are making between their own knowledge and experiences and the text. Through small-group discussion, teachers can guide pupils to make these connections and build up their ability to make logical inferences and predictions.

Although having access to high-quality, ambitious children's literature is very beneficial for all children, pupils in key stages 1 and 2 must have regular opportunities to practise reading books at their own instructional level (90–94% accuracy). Group guided reading provides a setting for texts that are pitched appropriately, and opportunities for adults to support readers in their word reading as well as their comprehension.

Concerns about group guided reading

Group guided reading often comes under scrutiny for how it is implemented. It's lovely to work with a group of six children, but what about the other 24? For this strategy to be effective, the children not working with an adult need to be (a) on task and (b) doing a high-quality, meaningful activity. Behaviour expectations and routines are key. Take time to develop a clear routine. Choose activities that are engaging and manageable without an adult present. Most importantly, give children opportunities to *read*. The group that has just read with the teacher the day before may benefit from a follow-up task that has already been explained. Other groups may pre-read ahead of their session with the teacher, read their own books independently or read other books linked to the class topic, whole-class novel or guided reading text.

My view

The conclusion to this debate is not an either / or answer. Teachers need to think about their setting and class, and the needs of their pupils. In doing so, they can choose a combination of effective teaching strategies that meet the needs of children at specific times.

Whole-class teaching is pacey and relies on a lot of direct-teaching methods. Teachers should look for ways to add variety to the school day, to help manage the stamina of all involved. Sometimes the focus on whole-class reading is the best option while, at other times, the quieter, more relaxed structure of group guided reading changes the pace and provides a different kind of learning.

Rewarding readers: managing home reading

There is no denying that children who develop the habit of reading widely and often not only become better readers but also achieve more highly across the curriculum. Good readers become good writers by internalising the rhythm and flow of language, building a large vocabulary and widening their life experiences through the books they read.

So how can schools encourage children (and parents or carers) to read at home?

For many years, a reading record or journal that is signed by a parent and collected each morning has become a habit in schools. This system relies on parents remembering to complete them and the labour-intensive job of checking them at school each day. When a reward or consequence is added to the expectation of bringing them to and from school, these reading records add unneeded stress for families and put more emphasis on the signature than the actual quality of the reading activities taking place. Reading soon turns from a pleasure to a chore.

Schools must also be mindful of the books children have available to them for home reading. Not everyone has shelves full of books to enjoy. Teachers must help children select appropriate books from the reading scheme, as well as from the school or class library. Visiting the local library to enable children to sign up for a library card and learn how to sign out books is also an important step in giving them access to a variety of books. Be sure to include information for parents about how to access the library.

Concerns about reading records and rewards

The following strategies will help support the effective monitoring of reading:

- If your school wants to use reading records, be mindful of attaching any rewards or consequences to whether or not it has been signed by a parent or carer. Instead, focus on using the records as a way for children to reflect on their reading or for parents to communicate with school about what has been read.
- In Years 5 and 6, encourage children to become reflective readers by looking after their own reading records. They could fill them in as they arrive in school, creating a lovely chatter about what they are reading. Higher-level teaching assistant and school librarian Nicki Cleveland says, 'As independent readers, we ask our Year 5 and 6 children to sign their own reading diaries, and tell us something about what they have read. It may be their favourite part, something that surprised them, new words, great phrases or an amazing fact. They can even tell us if they didn't enjoy what they read, as that's just as valid an opinion' (Cleveland, 2024).
- Give children time to talk about what they've read at home (so reading does not become a writing task). Pairs or small groups could share something about their current book and get recommendations.
- Strive to build a community of readers, as outlined in the Open University Reading for Pleasure initiative (see 'Further reading').
- Celebrate parents reading to their children as much as children reading to their parents. Encourage families to choose high-quality children's novels or non-fiction that children may not be able to read themselves.

Alternatives to reading records

Book talk

Give pupils time to talk in pairs or groups about what they've been reading. This might be independent reading at home or at school. Provide prompt cards with thought-provoking questions to get them chatting.

Reading challenges

Instead of having a reading log signed, give pupils a selection of fun reading challenges to complete at home with their books. These could be listed on a bookmark for children to colour in when complete, a 'bingo card' or a list. Challenges could include reading specific types of books or activities to do with their books. For example:

- read about another country
- read in every room in your house
- read a brochure or menu
- read in an unusual location
- read about an influential woman
- read while cuddling your pet
- read on an electronic device
- read after a bath or shower.

Reading bookmarks

These could be used to list reading challenges, or for parents simply to initial each time their child reads at home (see 'Further reading').

Reading bookshelf

Provide pupils with a blank outline of books on a bookshelf (like the one in Figure 5.1). Each time they finish a book, they should write its title on the spine of one of the books (see 'Further reading').

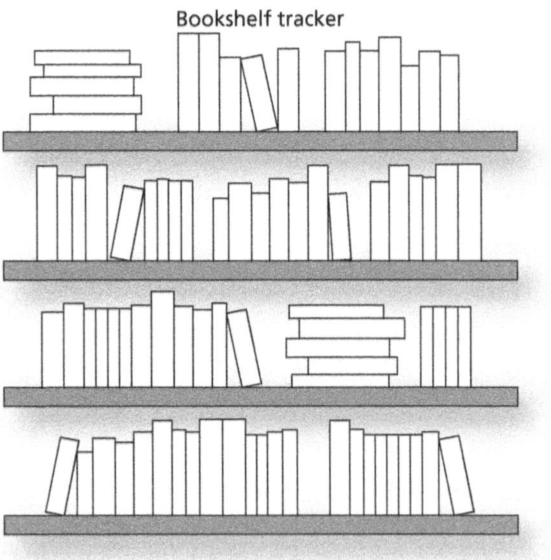

▲ **Figure 5.1 A blank bookshelf template can be motivating for pupils to fill in as they read**

Book journal or scrapbook

This could be a shared whole-class reading scrapbook that travels from house to house, or individual book journals in which children draw pictures and write quotations or opinions.

Reading tree

To make a reading tree, every time a pupil completes a book, they write their name and the book title on a paper leaf. Leaves are added to a class tree, so pupils can see their reading journey grow. At the end of the year, leaves may be returned to children, so they are reminded of what they've read (see 'Further reading').

Read whole novels together

Invest in class sets of novels, so every child has a book. Read to the pupils, ask them to read aloud, give them opportunities to read in groups and independently. Enjoy the whole book together.

Reading buddies

Partner with another class and give children opportunities to read aloud to each other. When a younger class pairs with an older class, there are so many opportunities to develop positive relationships and support each other throughout the year.

Padlet or Google Drive

Create an online reading wall where children and staff can post about what they're reading and leave comments for others.

Book vlogs

Pupils could create video blogs of their recent read, with a short description or opinion.

Reading conferences

Meet with each pupil to chat about what they've been reading and their reading interests, make book recommendations and set reading targets. Get to know children as readers.

My view

Our aim is to help develop motivated readers who find pleasure in books. For children to become lifelong readers, we need to concentrate on intrinsic motivation rather than ticks and stickers or winning prizes.

Someone who loves to read explores worlds and adventures within the pages of a book they choose because they want to, not because they have to.

Traditional spelling tests

Are spelling tests an effective way to improve spelling? Learning a list of words for a weekly test is a strategy that has been used for generations and is still widely used today – including in national assessments. There are spelling patterns, high-frequency words and statutory lists for children to learn, but what approach should we take and how should they be assessed?

The benefits of traditional spelling tests

Those in favour of spelling tests may argue that regular spelling tests motivate children to practise and learn their spellings, as they are encouraged to revise. Some children will become better spellers over time if they are able to transfer their rote learning of words to practical application in day-to-day writing. Spelling tests are most effective for the learning of irregular words that do not follow typical spelling patterns.

When teachers are sure of the purpose of giving the test and how the results will be used, spelling tests can be helpful. They give teachers information about the attainment and progress of their pupils, which will, in turn, allow them to adjust their teaching accordingly and identify children who need further support (Spell Wizards, 'Spelling tests: are they effective?').

Parents tend to like spelling tests because it is what they're used to from their own school days and it is something they can help with practically at home. They are able to encourage their children to memorise the spellings without having to understand the patterns themselves.

Concerns about traditional spelling tests

In reality, many children find spelling tests stressful. This anxiety may cause them to perform poorly, and create negative feelings towards spelling and writing more generally. This may be the case for children regardless of whether they are good spellers or find it difficult. The pressure to maintain a strong score or to achieve well when one doesn't find rote learning easy can cause dread as the weekly test approaches.

Spelling test results are often linked to the effort put in by the parent and child at home, away from school learning (Jago, 2021). This leaves some children distinctly disadvantaged and puts an extra element of pressure on children from well-meaning parents (Moorhead, 2021). Taking parents out of the equation gives a clearer picture of children's abilities and reduces anxiety.

Managing spelling tests in the classroom can be tricky. With a range of abilities, there may be differentiated lists to deliver. This results in lots of list-making and photocopying, as well as the logistics of testing everyone on their specific words (Jago, 2021). If just one class list is set, stronger spellers may not be stretched, while those who need more support will end up with a low score. This results in a cycle of some children always doing well and others always doing poorly.

Children may also experience the 'Friday test, Monday miss' phenomenon – they are able to spell words correctly for the test then are not able to apply those same spellings to their daily spelling the following week (Putnam, 2017). This happens because children have used rote learning to memorise the spellings. They do not understand why words are spelled in a particular way, because they have not taken the time to learn patterns and how words develop. They have not made use of prior knowledge of spelling patterns to build up spelling knowledge and make links between words.

The alternative to spelling tests

In her article 'Why I ditched the school spelling test' (2021), teacher Ann Jago explores an alternative to the rote learning of a weekly spelling test. She suggests three strategies that help children to learn both high-frequency words and spelling patterns in a kind, supportive environment.

1. **Word of the week:** Focus on one word. Consider its origin, think about word families, word class and syllables, play games with it and apply it to writing.
2. **Sentence dictation with high-frequency words:** Practise spelling high-frequency words through sentence dictation. Give everyone the same sentence: higher-attaining children are marked on the entire sentence, while lower-attaining children are marked only on the focus word. All learning and revision is done in class.
3. **Spelling patterns:** Spelling lessons focus on a specific pattern. Explore exceptions, common misspellings and the meaning of words. Revisit the pattern over the next number of weeks in plenaries or retrieval practice.

My view

Building a classroom culture of spelling where there is less fear and more interest in words means everyone has the chance to explore the English language and experience success. I believe traditional spelling tests are not a weekly requirement but better suited to less frequent summative assessment. Our time would be better spent using more formative assessment strategies to look at errors pupils are making in their individual writing, and addressing those needs. Pupils can be challenged to choose more ambitious vocabulary from new spelling patterns and apply their spelling lessons in real writing experiences.

Further reading

Jago, A. (2021) 'Why I ditched the school spelling test'. *TES*, www.tes.com/magazine/teaching-learning/primary/why-i-ditched-school-spelling-test

Open University, Reading for Pleasure, ourfp.org; specific details of the Reading for Pleasure pedagogy at https://ourfp.org/reading-for-pleasure-pedagogy/

Reading bookmarks, reading bookshelf, reading tree: for details of how to use these, see Clements, J., 'Reading record – download & alternative ideas for primary'. Teachwire, www.teachwire.net/teaching-resources/reading-records/

CHAPTER 6
SUBJECT-SPECIFIC RESEARCH

Research has informed my career far more than I could have imagined. This chapter will provide you with an overview of a handful of organisations, surveys and reports that I keep going back to, and explain why each is worthy of your time.

In Chapters 1, 2 and 3, I describe what effective teaching of spoken language, reading and writing looks like in practice. The pedagogical ideas in those chapters are grounded in research. This chapter will introduce you to the studies and surveys that underpin them. Consider it the evidence base behind the rest of the book. Each section includes enough information to help you judge whether the key claims are supported by data, but it also allows you to choose your own adventure – to follow whichever links seem most relevant to your practice.

A few notes on how to use this chapter: Think of it less as a reading list and more as a menu; no one has time to read every report in detail. Use your instinct about which organisation might be able to answer your current question – whether that's representation in your book corner, falling levels of enjoyment in Year 5 writing or a growing set of books to mark.

Where to find research on primary English

The following organisations have become trusted fixtures in my professional life. Each offers freely available reports, webinars and classroom resources written with primary teachers in mind.

Centre for Literacy in Primary Education (CLPE)

The Centre for Literacy in Primary Education is a UK-based children's literacy charity working with primary schools. Its aim is to raise the achievement of children's reading and writing by helping schools to teach literacy creatively and effectively, putting quality children's books at the heart of all learning. The CLPE offer includes both in-person and online CPD, and a website overflowing with free resources for teachers. See https://clpe.org.uk

Education Endowment Foundation (EEF)

The Education Endowment Foundation is an independent charity supporting educational establishments for children aged 2–19 years old. The EEF is dedicated to breaking the link between family income and education achievement by helping schools, nurseries and colleges to improve teaching and learning through better use of evidence. See https://educationendowmentfoundation.org.uk

United Kingdom Literacy Association (UKLA)

The United Kingdom Literacy Association is made up of thousands of teachers, educators, consultants, librarians and leading literacy researchers. It combines this considerable practical and professional experience with extensive knowledge of literacy research to support the development of effective literacy policy and provision. See https://ukla.org

Open University: Reading for Pleasure

Open University research has shaped a Reading for Pleasure movement that seeks to enable teachers to enrich their knowledge and practice, schools to create cultures of reading and stronger links with parents and young readers who benefit from being members of vibrant reading communities. See https://ourfp.org/reading-for-pleasure-pedagogy/

National Literacy Trust (NLT)

The National Literacy Trust is an independent charity that focuses on the importance of literacy in empowering individuals. It believes literacy holds the tools to success and opens doors to a more promising future. See https://literacytrust.org.uk

Research on representation and reading culture

CLPE 'Reflecting Realities': survey of ethnic representation within UK children's literature

Every year I go back to this report and share it because it matters so much. Commissioned and funded by Arts Council England, this annual survey covers the breadth and quality of representation of characters from marginalised ethnic groups in picture books, fiction and non-fiction published for children aged 3–11 years old in the UK. This year we have eight years of data, which lets us identify trends instead of snapshots

– trends that have impact when we're choosing books to put in front of children year after year.

So why does this research matter so much for our classrooms? When children are able to see themselves reflected in the books they read, they feel seen and valued. When they read about characters who share their experiences, they also read about their peers whose lives may look different from theirs, building empathy. For children who don't get to see a lot of diversity in their day-to-day lives, seeing different types of characters expands their worldview. The books on our classroom shelves silently send messages to children about who stories are for – and that extends to whether they believe those stories are for them.

Key findings from the eighth report (CLPE, 2025) include:

- Overall representation has rebounded after the previous year's sharp fall: 24% of reviewed children's books published in 2024 feature a character from a marginalised ethnic group, up from 17% in 2023, though still short of the 30% reached in 2022.
- Most strikingly, 24% of books now feature a main character from a marginalised ethnic group – the highest figure CLPE has ever reported, and a remarkable jump from 7% the previous year.
- Fiction has improved from 11% to 18%, and non-fiction from 22% to 27% – both welcome gains, though neither has yet returned to 2022 levels.
- Picture books, long the strongest of the three text types, saw their first reported drop, falling from 55% to 38%. They remain the highest-performing category, but the trend bears watching.

The CLPE's call to the publishing industry, to remain steadfast in producing inclusive, representative literature as standard practice rather than as a passing initiative, is one I would extend to teachers too. The books we choose, recommend and celebrate in our classrooms send a signal back to publishers about what readers want.

Reflecting on the importance of this work in the CLPE's 2024 report (CLPE, 2025), Dr Zaahida Nabagereka – a champion of diversity and inclusion in children's literature – warned that a failure to create nuanced, authentic representations of characters of colour risks reinforcing the idea that storytelling belongs only to a select few.

The CLPE publishes a new 'Reflecting Realities' report each November. I encourage you to check its website for the most recent edition and the curated booklists that accompany it – these are an excellent starting point for diversifying a class library.

Open University: Teachers as Readers

The Open University has been working with teachers and analysing their findings for a number of years. In 2008, the idea of primary teachers as readers themselves became a key part of the Reading for Pleasure initiative.

Teachers' knowledge of children's literature and other texts

The Teachers as Readers research project found that teachers need a wide and up-to-date knowledge of children's literature and other texts. This knowledge allows teachers to engage enthusiastically as readers with both pupils and other staff, setting an example of positive reading experiences and opening up conversation about books and reading habits. These reader-teachers are able to make thoughtful book recommendations and informed choices for texts to use in lessons and to read aloud to their class. They are able to create enriching learning experiences and foster a love of literature (Open University, c).

Teachers' knowledge of children's reading practices

The Teachers as Readers project also revealed that the more teachers know about children's reading life outside of school, the better they are able to nurture reading for pleasure and build a community of readers. As they come to know more about children's interests and reading preferences, they are able to tailor their recommendations and the types of reading experiences provided at school. Teachers are encouraged to broaden the definition of what counts as reading (including texts such as graphic novels and wider non-fiction). As teachers recognise and value the wide range of reading experiences and choices children make, they will be able to offer a more satisfying and diverse range of texts in school, and to foster positive reading identities for all children. This reading relationship is key to continuing to support a community of readers and encourage reading for pleasure for all (Open University, c).

CLPE 'What We Know Works' series

The CLPE has created a series of resources that pull together strategies and teaching ideas gathered from teachers working with them on their classroom-based research projects. With clear headlines and practical actions, these publications allow teachers to learn from research and choose new techniques that will work for them and their classes (CLPE, 2016).

The 'What We Know Works' series includes:

- 'Choosing and Using Quality Children's Texts'
- 'Poetry in Primary Schools'
- 'Reading for Pleasure'
- 'Writing in Primary Schools'.

If you are unsure where to start, I would begin with 'Choosing and Using Quality Children's Texts', which underpins the other three.

Research on writing

National Literacy Trust Annual Literacy Survey

This report explores children's and young people's writing enjoyment at school and in their free time. The headline figure shows that enjoyment of writing is at one of its lowest levels since 2010, with fewer than 3 in 10 (28.7%) reporting that they enjoy writing in their free time.

In 2023, the National Literacy Trust declared a writing-for-pleasure crisis, yet there continued to be a sharp decline in 2024 and a decline of 12.2% over 13 years.

The report (Clark et al, 2024) found that one in nine children (11.1%) who participated in the survey write daily in their free time. Of those who write at least once a month:

- three in five write to express their creativity
- one in two write to express their ideas and imagination
- one in two write to express their thoughts and feelings
- two in five write to relax
- one in three write to feel happier.

This research shines a light on the necessity of the Writing for Pleasure pedagogy, and the importance of teachers having time and resources to invest in children as writers. Continue to check back with the National Literacy Trust each year for the most up-to-date research.

UKLA: What is it Writing for Pleasure teachers do that makes the difference?

Writing for Pleasure in the classroom involves the teaching of writing associated with:

- high levels of pupil motivation (I know why)
- self-efficacy (I can)
- agency (I have a say)
- self-regulation (I know what to do and how to do it)
- volition (I want to)
- writer identity (I am)
- pleasure in writing (enjoyment and satisfaction).

Ross Young and UKLA spent a year studying the impact of implementing a Writing for Pleasure pedagogy and which strategies were particularly successful (Young, 2019). This research observed teaching of writing that is highly effective with children, resulting in greater than average progress. Children felt great enjoyment and satisfaction in writing and in being a writer. The findings showed that agency was very important to children as writers, but also that it must be supported by self-efficacy and self-regulation. This combination of factors increased motivation and children's ability to see themselves as writers. Although the classes involved in this research had great success and really grew in their writing for pleasure, there was still some way to go in fully developing their motivation for writing and writer-identity. All in all, the Writing for Pleasure pedagogy was found to be highly effective.

The research pinpoints a cluster of principles practised by Writing for Pleasure teachers: read, share and talk about writing; teach the writing processes explicitly; balance composition with transcription; establish a community of writers; set up meaningful, authentic writing projects; pupil conferencing; and… be a writer-teacher yourself. In my experience, 'be a writer-teacher' is the most difficult, and the most powerful, of these. It requires teachers to share their own drafts, talk about their own compositional challenges and model writing as process rather than product. If you're planning to read one Writing for Pleasure research article and want my tip for where to start, start here.

Research on literacy across the primary phase: the EEF guidance reports

Between them, the EEF's 'Improving literacy in key stage 1' (2020) and 'Improving literacy in key stage 2' (2021) guidance reports amount to the closest thing primary teachers have to a single-volume summary of the best available evidence on how to teach literacy.

Instead of listing all the recommendations here, I'd instead encourage you to download the reports and read through the top-line actions, along with the examples of practice that accompany them. What makes each report genuinely usable, however, is the way that this information is layered: there are short and snappy headline recommendations for those who are time-poor, further detail for those who want to dig deeper and even a poster you can print off and stick up in the staffroom.

What I recommend busy teachers do

As I set out at the start of this chapter, I want to provide you with a menu rather than a reading list. Here is my advice for interacting with research in primary English:

- Choose one organisation – CLPE, EEF, NLT or Open University – and follow it. Sign up to its newsletter and read it. Over the course of a year you will learn more than you would from a week of intensive research.
- Twice yearly, take a look at the latest 'Reflecting Realities' statistics and the NLT annual literacy survey. Let them prompt one honest discussion with your team about reading in your classrooms / school.
- Read one piece of EEF guidance from beginning to end. Just one. Then refer back to it when you are planning CPD / reviewing provision, etc.
- Locate one article on Writing for Pleasure research that resonates with you and pass it on to your team. Discussion about research often has more impact on practice than individual reading.
- Research should inform practice – not take too much time from it. The organisations and resources discussed above are the ones I have found most consistently achieve the former.

CHAPTER 7
PLANNING FOR PRIMARY ENGLISH

Planning is one of the core skills of effective teaching, but it works best when it's designed for the teacher using it, not just for paperwork. A good plan should act as a clear, supportive guide, built around meaningful prompts that help you map out progression and keep pupils moving towards the lesson objectives. Rather than being overly detailed or time-consuming, it should strike a balance – capturing key learning steps, questions and adaptations without becoming more onerous than the teaching itself. When planning is purposeful and manageable, it frees you to focus on responsive teaching, ensuring lessons stay engaging, structured and impactful for every pupil.

So far, we have looked at what is involved in teaching primary English – the spoken language, reading and writing strands in the national curriculum, plus the research that tells us how pupils learn these three strands most effectively. Planning pulls all these strands together. It's how you turn the national curriculum's legal requirements into logical year-by-year teaching, and then into topic sequences and daily lessons.

In this chapter, we will examine that process at four distinct levels. Each plan type is nested within the next: whole-school progression map, long-term curriculum map, medium-term topic-sequence plan and short-term lesson plan. We'll start at the top because it's necessary to work from these plans in sequence. The joy of good planning is that, by the time you're teaching the lesson, a lot of the hard thinking has already been done.

Progression maps: whole-school plans

Progression maps for English show how knowledge and skills are developed year to year: road maps for learning, they ensure everyone clearly understands what should be taught and how pupils will progress as they move through school. When these objectives have been carefully plotted in a logical sequence, lessons build naturally on prior learning, creating opportunities for success.

Clear, focused progression maps form the backbone of planning. They allow teachers to devise age-appropriate lessons, identify any gaps in previous learning and adapt teaching as necessary. Developing school-wide progression maps means teachers are not trying to create long-term plans for themselves, and everyone is focused on the same aims. Teachers are then able to use the objectives on the progression map to inform their topic sequences and ultimately their daily lesson plans.

Progression map (school overview)	→	Curriculum map (long-term plans)	→	Topic sequence (medium-term plans)	→	Lesson plans (short-term plans)

Rather than one huge progression map for all of primary English, many schools create smaller, more manageable documents for each area: reading, writing and spoken language. Some also create progression maps for grammar, punctuation, spelling and even handwriting.

Schools may also choose to create progression maps for the text types pupils will revisit as they move through school. Having clear expectations for what instruction texts, non-chronological reports or recounts will look like in Year 1, Year 2 and onwards all the way to Year 6 ensures teachers plan lessons that provide challenge and new learning, while pupils build on previous lessons.

The starting point for creating progression maps is the national curriculum (DfE, 2013b). It states what pupils are expected to be able to do as they reach the end of each key stage or year. In primary English, these objectives are listed for key stage 1 (Years 1 and 2), lower key stage 2 (Years 3 and 4) and upper key stage 2 (Years 5 and 6). The combination of year groups in key stage 2 means schools need to spend time breaking down the objectives and creating benchmarks for learning for each year group. It may be that schools in your local authority or trust have already done some work on this, which might be shared.

Some commercial schemes bundle progression maps with an assessment system that allows teachers to identify whether pupils are working at, below or above age-related expectations. They can be a useful shortcut, especially for schools that lack the resources to create their own maps from scratch. The downside is that a ready-made map will be based on its publisher's priorities rather than those of your school, so it's worth amending rather than adopting outright.

The CLPE has created Reading and Writing Scales that describe the journey children take on the path to becoming more literate (CLPE, 2015–16). Designed with progress in mind, teachers may use these scales to identify the current abilities of the pupils they teach and gain understanding of clear next steps. From beginner through to maturity and independence, these scales help teachers identify which opportunities and objectives to provide for their pupils. The 'Next Steps' sections of these documents are invaluable in providing teachers with clear actions that will help children progress along the scale.

Many schools choose to take the objectives from the national curriculum and create their own progression maps that focus on the priorities of their school and meet the needs of the pupils they teach. Investing time in writing bespoke progression maps is a valuable experience that allows subject leaders and class teachers really to immerse themselves in what pupils need to learn and how each experience builds on what has come before. Having a cohesive progression map ensures there are no gaps in learning, avoids repetition and pupils enter each new year group with the learning they need to be successful as they move through school. This is not to say teachers do not revisit learning from previous year groups. It allows them to understand what to revise, where to focus the learning and how to provide extension. A clear progression map creates a shared responsibility for children's learning and goes some way to alleviating the pressure that can fall on teachers in the Year 2 and Year 6 statutory assessment year groups.

Here are my suggested steps for creating progression maps for primary English:

1 Work as a team with experience from across the school.
2 Working together, identify school priorities (e.g. reading for pleasure, reading for empathy, writing for an audience or writing with purpose). These will be the threads that run through your whole-school progression map. They will enhance the basic objectives and bring purpose to your plans.
3 Identify the key areas of learning that will be mapped across all year groups in your progression map (e.g. 'phonics and decoding' in reading, 'awareness of audience' in writing or 'asking and answering questions' in spoken language).
4 Identify and track learning objectives for each phase: EYFS, key stage 1, lower key stage 2 and upper key stage 2. Make sure each statement builds on what has come before. The national curriculum will provide the basis for many of these statements, but remember to add your own priorities and focus.

5 Once the learning for each phase has been established, break those statements down for each year group. What needs to be learned in Year 3 that bridges the gap between the Year 2 objectives and what needs to be secure by the end of Year 4? Complete the same process for Year 5. These are key year groups for consolidating prior learning and laying the foundation for end-of-phase outcomes.

6 Think carefully about common misconceptions and areas of learning that tend to be particularly difficult. Track them through the year groups. Where do misconceptions lie? How can you build in more support early on, so children experience success?

7 Plan for repetition, revision and reflection. Ensure pupils have the opportunity to consolidate learning and are not just rushing from one learning objective to the next.

8 Give all teachers the opportunity to check the progression map and give feedback. Discuss any areas of concern, balancing the demands of the national curriculum with your knowledge of your own pupils.

9 Remember that just identifying the texts you will use in each year group is not a curriculum plan. These texts may change as better choices are discovered / published, a particular class cannot access a text due to personal circumstances or the text does not age well and becomes problematic. The curriculum plan should be built around learning objectives and the needs of the pupils.

On the next page is an example of an extract from a reading progression map. It shows progression in the key area of 'making inferences'. I've chosen this strand for two reasons: first, because it consistently develops throughout each year group, making the progression arc clear to see; and, second, because it's a helpful illustration of how a school can use national curriculum objectives as a starting point and develop year-by-year expectations that focus on progress and clearly demonstrate what you want children to achieve. This is one of the most useful functions of a whole-school map.

Table 7.1 Making inferences

Reading	EYFS	Key stage 1		Lower Key Stage 2		Upper Key Stage 2	
		Year 1	Year 2	Year 3	Year 4	Year 5	Year 6
Making inferences	Details of objectives for: • three- and four-year-olds • Reception • Early Learning Goals	Listen to and discuss a wide range of poems, stories and non-fiction at a level beyond that at which they can read independently Be encouraged to link what they read or hear read to their own experiences Draw on what they already know or on background information provided by the teacher Make simple inferences based on characters' feelings, words and actions Look for clues in words and illustrations	Listen to, discuss and express views about a wide range of contemporary and classic poetry, stories and non-fiction at a level beyond that at which they can read independently Draw on what they already know or on background information provided by the teacher Make inferences about feelings, thoughts and character motive based on feelings, words and actions Look for evidence in words, whole sentences and illustrations	Listen to and discuss a wide range of fiction, poetry, plays, non-fiction and reference books or textbooks Read books that are structured in different ways and read for a range of purposes Ask questions to improve understanding of a text Make inferences about characters' feelings, thoughts and motives from their actions and relationships with others Justify inferences with evidence from words, sentences and across a paragraph	Listen to and discuss a wide range of fiction, poetry, plays, non-fiction and reference books or textbooks Read books that are structured in different ways and read for a range of purposes Ask questions to improve understanding of a text Make more developed inferences about emotions, behaviour and relationships Justify inferences with evidence from words, sentences, across a paragraph and from different parts of the text	Continue to read and discuss an increasingly wide range of fiction, poetry, plays, non-fiction and reference books or textbooks Read books that are structured in different ways and read for a range of purposes Ask questions to improve understanding Make considered inferences about characters' feelings, thoughts and motives from their words and actions including viewpoints and character development More precisely justify inferences with specific evidence from words, sentences, across a paragraph and from different parts of the text Explain how an author's language choices contribute to inference	Continue to read and discuss an increasingly wide range of fiction, poetry, plays, non-fiction and reference books or textbooks Read books that are structured in different ways and read for a range of purposes Ask questions to improve understanding Make sophisticated inferences about characters' feelings, thoughts and motives from their words and actions within the context of themes of the text Consider multiple interpretations and contrasting evidence Expertly justify inferences with quotes from across the whole text while making connections and evaluating evidence Explain authorial intentions and impact on the reader with regards to inference

Curriculum maps: long-term plans

Before moving from progression maps to topic sequences, schools must develop a clear curriculum map. This will ensure all teachers know what they need to teach each half-term and there are no gaps or repetition. Essentially, the curriculum map is the long-term plan for each year group in each subject, focusing on texts, genres and themes. It may contain opportunities for cross-curricular links as well as links to the school's PSHCE or ethos focus. Primary English is no longer constructed around writing text types, but these may be included in curriculum maps so English leads can be certain pupils are experiencing a range.

Many schools create a spiral curriculum map that allows pupils to revisit and extend key areas of learning. For example, Year 1 pupils may write a letter to Granny warning her that the Big Bad Wolf has been spotted in the forest. In Year 3, pupils revisit letter-writing to ask the PTA for funds to buy sports equipment. In Year 6, pupils could further extend their letter-writing skills by writing to their MP about an environmental issue. Each time, the letters are more sophisticated, make better use of typical features and have a very different purpose.

A school-wide curriculum map created in partnership with class teachers ensures there is no repetition of texts and all text selections are age and content appropriate. Revisiting these curriculum maps each year provides English leads with the opportunity to introduce new, high-quality books, and allows existing and new staff to suggest books they are passionate about. This keeps lessons fresh and up to date. It's important to remember that we are teaching the objectives not the text. The topic is not *War Horse* or *The Lighthouse Keeper's Lunch*; it is the reading, writing and spoken language objectives carried by those texts. The vehicle for the learning may change from time to time, but the journey is still the same. On the flip side of this, it is important that texts do not change too often (or there are too many changes in one year), to prevent increased workload for teachers planning lessons.

Curriculum maps may come from a bought-in scheme or be devised in-house. If schools choose to create their own curriculum maps, they are able to cherry-pick the best resources and use the talents and creativity of their own teachers to create plans that really meet the needs of their pupils. Balancing this with a mindfulness of workload and the many fantastic resources available, schools may also choose to use curriculum maps (and the accompanying plans) from organisations such as CLPE Power of Reading, and many others.

The Table 7.2 template organises a year group's English curriculum across the six half-terms, with texts and authors providing a spine at the centre of each block, and reading, writing and language objectives branching off from these. I've adapted this template from the CLPE's English curriculum maps, which I've found offer a particularly useful framework for both new and seasoned subject leads; of course, the usefulness of any template will depend on how you adapt it to suit your needs.

Table 7.2 Sample framework for an English curriculum map (adapted from CLPE, English curriculum maps)

Year group:	**Autumn A**	**Autumn B**	**Spring A**	**Spring B**	**Summer A**	**Summer B**
	Topic title **Texts** **Authors**	**Topic title** **Texts** **Authors**	**Topic title** **Texts** **Authors**	**Topic title** **Texts** **Authors**	**Topic title** **Texts** **Authors**	**Topic title** **Texts** **Authors**
PSHCE / ethos Theme						
Cross-curricular links						
Literary forms (text types)						
Inspiration (hook)						
Reading objectives						
Writing objectives						
Vocabulary Grammar Punctuation						
Spelling						
Extended writing outcomes						

Topic sequences: medium-term plans

Topic sequences, or medium-term unit plans, pull together themes, objectives and ideas from progression maps and curriculum maps, turning them into a coherent series of lessons. This is not short-term planning, with each lesson completely fleshed out, but rather the tracking of the learning journey over a one- to four-week unit of work with headlines for each lesson.

Each primary English topic sequence should include the essentials: high-quality talk, developing vocabulary, opportunities to develop grammar and punctuation, modelling, many opportunities to write, meaningful feedback and an opportunity to respond to the feedback.

The basic topic sequence for primary writing follows these steps:

Read → Analyse → Write

It may also be described as:

Read → Discover → Practise → Apply

Opportunities to read, analyse and then write may occur multiple times within one teaching sequence, depending on the length of the unit, the needs of the pupils and the objectives being taught.

The basic sequence can be developed further with more detail:

1 Create interest or awe and wonder through a meaningful hook.
2 Introduce a model text.
   a) Read with a reader's eye: read for pleasure and consider how the text affects you.
   b) Read with a writer's eye: consider how the writer has achieved their aims, learn from their techniques and think about how to apply them to your own writing.
3 Understand the topic by thinking about context for writing: what is the purpose, who is the audience, what do I already know about text types I might use?
4 Capture ideas, learn the skills, practise, plan, have a go.
5 Write: teacher modelling, planning, drafting, editing, redrafting.

List adapted from NATE Primary Matters (2020)

Each of these stages deserves a closer look, but let's start where every good unit starts – with the hook. As the moment that sets the tone for everything that follows, it's worth giving it some real thought.

Meaningful hooks

A hook is when a teacher creates awe and wonder through an engaging stimulus or activity. The aim is to grab children's attention and encourage them to feel excited about the upcoming lesson or topic. These hooks may activate a child's background knowledge, promote thinking and generate questions. Hooks bring fun and a sense of play to the lesson, while creating a memorable shared experience for the class.

Lesson or topic hooks can be as simple or as elaborate as you wish. They may be quite small, like a prop, video clip or letter, but they may also be quite elaborate and require a bit more planning.

Ideas for hooks

- **Video:** Use a short video clip linked to the topic: find one online, make your own or use one of the excellent videos linked to English on the Literacy Shed website (www.literacyshed.com). You may want to produce a movie-trailer-type video to give a preview of the topic. Megan Diede and Kara Rigsby give an example of this in their blog post '25 engaging lesson hooks' (Diede and Rigsby, 2021).
- **Text:** Use a short picture book, poem, fiction extract or non-fiction text to capture children's interest. Choose something with a strong emotional response (funny, scary, touching) or unique interest to prompt children to respond.
- **Discussion:** Start the lesson with a question that will prompt strong opinions. Give pupils time to think and respond, justifying their opinions with evidence. Use partner talk to build ideas and start a debate.
- **Photos:** Share an interesting photo. It could be of a character, setting or unusual item. Encourage children to ask questions about the photo and think carefully about the clues provided. Take your own photo, find one online or use the Pobble website (www.pobble.com), which provides a new, free image every day.
- **Props:** Share an unusual object linked to the topic. Encourage children to make inferences about where it came from and to whom it belonged.
- **Mystery box / bag:** Share a box or bag full of unusual objects. Ask children to help take them out one by one, making inferences as they

discover each object. Encourage them to make connections between the objects and think about possible owners.

- **Story bag:** Introduce a bag of items all linked to a story. Make predictions about the character, setting and plot. Use the bag as you tell the story.
- **Message / letter:** Reveal a message or letter from a character. It might instruct the children to do something, share some important information or introduce a mystery.
- **Map:** Discover a map of a real or imaginary place. Encourage children to look closely, ask questions and try to work out the location.
- **Creative activities:** Make links to art and design to introduce a topic. Use creative resources such as modelling clay, painting or collage to explore new ideas.
- **Music:** Play a piece of music to create atmosphere. Talk about the feelings linked to the music and how it helps to set atmosphere.
- **Lighting:** Use lighting to create atmosphere – dim the lights, use a spotlight, fill the room with battery-powered tea lights, use a crackling fireplace video on-screen or use side lamps.
- **Costumes and fabrics:** Use textiles to set the scene and inspire a role. Costumes help everyone to step into their imagination. When hot-seating, a chair covered with a special piece of fabric can magically change an ordinary person into a character.
- **Visualisation:** Ask children to close their eyes as you guide them through a visualisation. Introduce story elements, plot structure or characters they will be able to use in their own writing later.
- **Online author visit:** This works well at the beginning or towards the end of a topic when children know more about the books. Help children prepare with good-quality questions and an awareness of the author. An author is a very powerful role model for writing.
- **Drama activities:** Use hot-seating, freeze frame or teacher-in-role to bring children right into the action. Encourage deeper thinking, questioning and prediction as they direct the drama.
- **Drama workshop:** Find a large space to explore a new topic in role. Perhaps you are a group of townspeople who are unhappy with a proposal to build a wind farm, or passengers about to set off on a trip to Greece on a plane. Exploring dialogue, actions and feelings in role will inspire writing.

- **Go on an adventure:** Plan an educational visit, send children on a quest across the playground following maps and clues to solve a mystery, create a scavenger hunt with clues linked to the topic or use virtual-reality headsets to explore something new.
- **Theme day:** Plan an entire day of activities linked to your new English topic. Build in opportunities for reading, writing and a lot of spoken language. The theme could be linked to a text, a large writing project or even grammar objectives. Farsley Farfield Primary School's Year 6 Star Wars Day linked to using passive voice (complete with costumes) has always been a huge hit!

Discrete or embedded grammar and punctuation

There are numerous aspects of grammar and punctuation that need to be introduced and revisited throughout key stages 1 and 2. These lessons will have the most impact when taught in context and applied to the text with writing occurring throughout the teaching sequence. However, embedded grammar lessons must be meaningful and focused, or they run the risk of getting lost in everything else children are being asked to juggle. At times, a discrete grammar or punctuation lesson may be needed, to give everyone time to grapple with concepts and learn to apply them correctly. Some schools choose to have a focused grammar lesson once each week linked to the text and the rest of the topic sequence. Others use lesson starters to revisit and revise previous grammar learning. In both cases, opportunities to apply this learning to real writing experiences are key. Finding a balance between discrete and embedded grammar and punctuation lessons will allow teachers to really focus on the terminology and provide children with opportunities to practise using these skills in different ways then apply what they've learned to their writing.

In *Teaching English by the Book* (2017), English consultant James Clements suggests what he terms a 'contextualised approach' – one that combines discrete and embedded methods. Clements believes grammar should be taught through the writing children read and write, but that they should always be made aware of how language functions and how specific choices affect meaning. Importantly, Clements includes accurate grammatical terminology in this 'explicitness' – children should not simply be effective users of language; they should also have a common language with which to discuss it.

There are many published programmes that provide teaching sequences for schools. Using the same scheme across school builds consistency, reduces teacher workload and can ensure the use of a solid teaching sequence with high-quality example texts. Some schemes are more focused on writing outcomes, while others pull reading and writing together into one cohesive sequence.

Big Writing by Ros Wilson (www.andrelleducation.com/big-writing), CLPE Power of Reading (https://clpe.org.uk/books/power-of-reading/about) and Talk for Writing (www.talk4writing.com) by Pie Corbett and Julia Strong are three well-known, researched-based approaches for topic sequences used by many schools around the UK. A number of other resources are also available.

Short-term lesson plans

Whichever approach a school adopts, planning eventually narrows down to the individual lesson, where long-term vision meets the reality of the classroom. The rest of this chapter turns to what makes a lesson genuinely effective, beginning with the structure of a writing lesson.

The structure of a writing lesson

Effective writing lessons have six key elements. The beauty of this structure is that these elements don't need to be taught in the same order in every lesson. Depending on the lesson's location within the wider teaching unit, the needs of the pupils and the objectives being taught, they can be rearranged into almost any order. This flexibility provides variety and motivation, while allowing teachers to guide pupils through an effective writing process and respond to needs and misconceptions as they arise.

The six key elements

1 **Aims of the session:** Identify the learning objectives to be achieved. Consider prior learning and where the writing unit is headed. Share a clear learning objective or aim with pupils at the beginning of the session, or reveal it as the learning occurs.

2 **Instruction:** Use direct and explicit instruction to teach a writing objective. This might include grammar concepts, writing techniques, focus on use of language or learning about author voice. This session could be a mini-lesson or a longer chunk of teaching time. Teachers

may use a model text or live modelling to demonstrate how pupils will apply their new learning to their own writing.

3 **Writing time:** Pupils need plenty of time to practise their writing, building confidence and developing their sense of themselves as writers. Not every piece of writing needs to be a huge undertaking. Shorter tasks provide opportunities to apply new techniques and experiment with structure and language. During writing time, be mindful of the amount of time pupils are able to write without a break. Pause their writing strategically to share good examples or to address a common misconception with a mini-lesson.
4 **Feedback:** Giving live feedback as pupils write is an incredibly powerful tool. Teachers are able to head off misconceptions and address learning gaps in the moment. Individual and small-group instruction provides support for children as they juggle all the skills required to be an effective writer.
5 **Class sharing:** After writing time, give pupils opportunities to share what they've achieved. This might be with a partner, a small group or in front of the class. Celebrate their writing and build them up as authors. A visualiser is a valuable tool for sharing children's writing. Using screen mirroring on a tablet also allows teachers to project children's writing onto the whiteboard. Give everyone an opportunity to give feedback, reflecting on what the writer has done well and where they can improve.
6 **Plenary:** Review what has been achieved and revisit the learning objective / lesson aim. Ask the pupils how they feel about the lesson. Do they need more time? Are there any questions or uncertainties? What do they need to know to make their writing even better?

Possible lesson structures

The Writing for Pleasure Centre shares a variety of possible lesson structures that include these key elements, demonstrating just how flexible teachers can be with their writing lessons (see Figure 7.1).

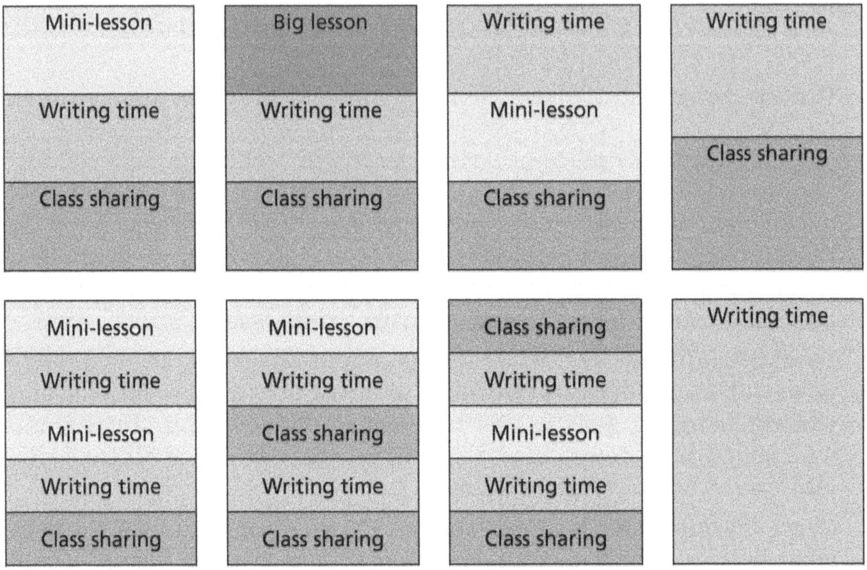

▲ **Figure 7.1 Example lesson structures (Writing for Pleasure Centre, 2022)**

On some days, more direct instruction is needed to develop new learning; on others, pupils need a good period of time to get on with their writing. Teachers may wish to let them write and focus on giving feedback to groups and individuals, or they may spot a common misconception that needs to be addressed. They can pause the writing time, bring pupils back together for a mini-lesson and then let them continue writing. Knowing the class and their stage in the writing process will help teachers choose the correct structure each day.

Discrete reading lessons

In many schools, it is common practice to teach reading lessons separately from the English lesson containing the writing teaching and outcomes. This may take the form of whole-class reading lessons or group guided reading. These are typically shorter lessons than the standard hour for English, often ranging from 20 to 45 minutes.

The focus of these lessons is purely on reading, rather than reading to develop writing, and will include:

- developing fluency
- accessing background knowledge

- comprehension
- reading for purpose
- reading for pleasure
- exposure to a range of texts.

The approach to this sequence of lessons will differ between schools, influenced by the teaching schemes being used, the needs of the pupils and preferences of the teacher.

Reading diet

It is essential children receive a varied diet of fiction, non-fiction, poetry, graphic novels and play scripts. These may come from longer books, short stories or extracts. Use of real-world resources, such as leaflets, magazines, newspapers, songs and online articles, will provide breadth and develop the understanding that reading is not just for school.

Teachers need to be cautious they aren't throwing too many different texts at pupils over the course of the week. Time to read, reread and digest a text builds fluency, solidifies understanding of vocabulary and deepens comprehension.

Companion texts are incredibly valuable. Finding a range of texts by the same author, on the same topic or with contrasting points of view helps pupils to make connections between what they are reading. This works well when making cross-curricular links with other subjects (for example, a geography topic about the Caribbean while reading *Clean Up!* by Nathan Bryon [author] and Dapo Adeola [illustrator], alongside poems from *Under the Moon & Over the Sea: A Collection of Caribbean Poems* by John Agard and Grace Nichols [editors]. Companion texts do not have to be linked to cross-curricular topics. Reading about Paddington Bear's arrival in London followed by a non-fiction text about Peru and a recipe for marmalade is just as meaningful.

Using the class novel

Often teachers will have a class novel they are reading aloud to pupils each day. This is a wonderful shared experience, allowing children to enjoy a book together and giving them access to high-quality books beyond their independent reading ability. It may be tempting to use the same book in reading lessons. This can be tricky, though, as it is difficult to predict exactly how far along in the book the class will be at a given time. It is possible to revisit an earlier extract from the class novel in a reading lesson, but switching from reading for pleasure to analysing the story can break the flow of the experience and change the focus. Some teachers believe it is better to save this class novel for pressure-free story time and use other texts for reading lessons.

Extracts versus whole books

Extracts taken from high-quality texts give children a taste of a variety of text types and genres. They are able to explore different structures, perspectives and styles of writing. Short texts allow readers to compare and contrast authors and form opinions on their preferences. When extracts are taken from real books, children will often be inspired to continue reading, finding books they might not otherwise discover. Teachers should be able to point children towards these books on the library shelf.

However, pupils cannot learn to read on a diet made up entirely of extracts. Experience with whole books allows readers to understand structure, plot, character development and themes. Understanding where a text comes from provides insight into the author's purpose and helps readers see the bigger picture. Children will encounter whole books through the class read-aloud novel, as the stimulus and model in English (writing) lessons and, on occasion, in reading lessons, either as a series of extracts from the same book or as a chapter-by-chapter study of a short novel or non-fiction book.

Choosing appropriate texts

Any texts used with children must be of the highest quality and appropriate for that particular cohort. Just because a certain book has always been used, doesn't mean it's the right one for that year. Schools sometimes fall into the trap of using a book because they happen to have a class set or because the planning is all done. Refreshing reading units is essential to allow for the use of better books with more learning opportunities and the inclusion of recent publications allowing for empathy building, diversity and inclusion, and widening worldviews.

Of course budget and teacher workload must be considered, but don't be afraid to make a change if it's the right choice for the children.

This checklist will help teachers consider whether a text is right for their class:

- Correct instructional level (90–94% accuracy for most pupils)
- Appropriate length for the intended lesson
- Enjoyable
- Contains an appropriate message or theme
- Any triggers or sensitive content have been considered
- Full of rich vocabulary
- Many opportunities for discussion, questioning and high-quality learning.

Jo Payne, deputy headteacher and author of the blog Mrs P Teach, recommends reading a book twice when planning a teaching unit. The first read is a simple one. Read for quality and enjoyment. Look for Big Ideas and main themes, while assessing the difficulty level. This is also the time to look out for sensitive content that may be a trigger for particular children.

The second read is where the detailed planning comes in. Make a list of key vocabulary. Which words need to be pre-taught? Which words will be studied in lessons? Which words are specific to the culture of the characters or linked to the topic? Consider the background knowledge required to understand the context of the book. Will children need experiences or exposure to certain ideas before reading? Spot key plot points to stop and summarise or make predictions. Identify the best extracts to be used in lessons (Mrs P Teach, 2021).

Question types

Reading comprehension is often broken up into different question types. This forms the basis of statutory assessment in England and can be used as a guide for teachers to ensure they ask a range of questions.

Key stage 1 (DfE, 2015a):

- vocabulary (knowledge of vocabulary to understand texts)
- retrieval (identify / explain key aspects of fiction and non-fiction texts, such as characters, events, titles and information)
- sequencing (identify and explain the sequence of events in texts)
- inference (make inferences from the text)
- prediction (predict what might happen on the basis of what has been read so far).

Key stage 2 (DfE, 2015b):

- vocabulary (give / explain the meaning of words in context)
- retrieval (retrieve and record information / identify key details from fiction and non-fiction)
- summarising (summarise main ideas from more than one paragraph)
- inference (make inferences from the text / explain and justify inferences with evidence from the text)
- prediction (predict what might happen from details stated and implied)
- text structure (identify / explain how information / narrative content is related and contributes to meaning as a whole)
- authors' use of language (identify / explain how meaning is enhanced through choice of words and phrases)
- comparison (make comparisons within the text).

These question types should not be taught entirely in isolation, as children use a combination of the skills involved when discussing a text and answering questions (for example, an understanding of vocabulary is required to discuss the author's use of language, while strong predictions grow out of the ability to make inferences and justify reasoning). However, asking a variety of good questions is a key part of teaching reading.

When developing questions, teachers should be led by the text. Look for the key tier two vocabulary required to understand and get the most out of the text. Identify the main facts children should be able to retrieve from the text. Look for opportunities for inference and prediction. Identify use of specific language features and interesting turns of phrase. Look for opportunities for children to make connections and comparisons as they uncover the overarching themes and messages of the text.

See Chapter 1 to learn more about tier two vocabulary.

Remember: questions during reading lessons are not an assessment. They prompt discussion and give pupils opportunities to think more deeply about the text. There may not be only one right answer. Give children time to think, share and revise their answers.

In my experience of teaching reading, some of the best questions are often the ones that come up on the spot. Following the pupils' train of thought and continuing to probe into their understanding will help them deepen that understanding and make meaningful connections. Don't be afraid to deviate from your plan and see where the discussion leads.

Teaching sequence for reading

There are many options for the structure of the teaching sequence for reading.

▼ **Table 7.3 One text across several lessons**

Lesson 1	Lesson 2	Lesson 3	Lesson 4
• Pre-reading activities and prediction • Use the cover, blurb and background knowledge • Build excitement and engagement • Focus on additional background knowledge required to understand the text • First reading of the text (independent or teacher read)	• Second reading of the text (modelled by the teacher with pupils following) • Look at key vocabulary and strategies for understanding vocabulary in context	• Third reading of the text (choose a reading style such as paired reading) • Discuss and write answers to a range of questions	• Final reading of the text (independent) • Discuss and write answers to a range of questions • Make connections to other texts, authors or areas of life (as a class, in groups or in pairs)

▼ **Table 7.4 Multiple texts across the week (Ashley Booth whole-class reading, Booth, 2020)**

Monday	Tuesday	Wednesday	Thursday	Friday
Reading lesson based on class novel	Linked text 1	Linked text 2	Linked text 3	Reading lesson based on class novel

Teacher Ashley Booth has created a teaching sequence for reading in key stage 2 covering the majority of the school year. He encourages teachers to use their class novel for reading lessons on Mondays and Fridays, leaving the other three days for stand-alone texts. These texts include extracts from core texts he believes children should have the opportunity to read during their time in primary, or may be linked by a theme. These themes include science, history and geography topics as well as PSHE focuses.

This resource is a goldmine, freely available for teachers to use and adapt for their own settings. This approach allows schools to balance the teaching of a whole novel with shorter extracts, many of which have been taken from high-quality whole books. Each lesson has been developed using a variety of question types.

Within the five-day structure, each lesson contains a 'Quick Start' activity involving retrieval, a 'Vocab Check' and opportunities for partner talk, individual thinking and solo work. A PowerPoint is available for each lesson, with questions prepared.

The structure of a reading lesson

Whether teaching whole-class reading lessons or small-group guided reading, the basic lesson structure is the same. There are seven key elements. Much like with writing lessons, the time spent on each of these elements will vary lesson to lesson to meet the needs of the class.

1. **Aims of the session:** Identify the learning objectives to be achieved. Consider prior learning and where the reading unit is headed. Share a clear learning objective or aim with children at the beginning of the session, or reveal it as the learning occurs. This objective or aim will come from curriculum requirements, the needs of the children and age-appropriate reading strategies.
2. **Book / text introduction (hook):** Spark interest in what the class will be reading through something as simple as an engaging introduction or as elaborate as a collection of related objects. Use photos, an intriguing headline, thought-provoking questions, a collection of key words or even the teacher acting in role to activate prior knowledge and capture children's imaginations. Enthusiasm about the lesson is key. A teacher's passion for reading is contagious.
3. **Mini-lesson:** The mini-lesson is a brief period of direct teaching. It could include the pre-teaching of key tier two vocabulary, the introduction of a specific reading strategy or revisiting an area of difficulty from a previous lesson. Examples of reading strategies include:
   - questioning
   - skimming and scanning
   - close reading

- predicting
- summarising
- activating prior knowledge
- inferring
- considering point of view and bias
- making comparisons
- identifying authors' use of language
- understanding text structure
- reading with purpose
- selecting relevant information
- understanding tables
- visualising
- making connections
- monitoring comprehension.

4 **Reading:** The core of any reading lesson is about giving pupils time to engage with the text. This will take a variety of forms and differ from lesson to lesson. It is essential that children are able to see the text, preferably their own copy. Reading techniques include:

- teacher-modelled reading as children follow along
- choral reading
- echo reading
- paired reading
- independent reading.

Be sure to include regular fluency practice as a part of these sessions.

5 **Reflection:** Before leaping into comprehension questions or a related task, give pupils time to reflect. What does this text mean to them personally? How do they feel about what they've read? This reflection may be personal thoughts, discussions in pairs, groups or the whole class, a written reflection (perhaps a reading journal) or drawing.

6 **Response:** Look deeper into the text. Using a variety of carefully crafted questions, discuss the text together. Pupils may write their answers or share orally. Complete activities linked to the text that develop comprehension, such as character profiles, summaries, tracking changes across a story or writing their own questions

about the text. These should be relatively short activities that can be completed within the 30–45-minute lesson.

7 **Follow-up task:** Sometimes a reading lesson needs to be extended to a full hour or linked to another session so children can complete longer activities that really deepen their understanding. These follow-up tasks may include developing written answers to questions discussed orally, creating comic strips of plot points or posters of the main theme, retelling a scene in role from a different point of view or writing a book review. These tasks must be meaningful and develop comprehension.

In summary

At its best, planning for primary English comes down to making decisions. Your whole-school progression map all the way down to your individual lesson plan exists to remove some of the thinking required of you at the point when you need to do most thinking: when you're in front of the class. If your progression map is clear, your curriculum map will fall into place. If your curriculum map is clear, your topic sequences will write themselves, and if your topic sequences are doing their job, then the lesson in front of you should be mostly about responding to your pupils, not reinventing the wheel.

CHAPTER 8
CORE READING SPINES

If you ask a group of adult readers which books from their childhood made them a reader, many of the same books and authors will come up again and again: *The Chronicles of Narnia*, *The Worst Witch*, *Meg and Mog*, Nancy Drew, A.A. Milne, Enid Blyton, Roald Dahl, E. Nesbit, Noel Streatfield... Fondly remembered, readers can still talk about the lessons they learned from these special books.

Which books are at the heart of your literary tradition? Which books do you expect (or hope) children will be familiar with as they move through school? Creating a reading spine (a list of core texts for pupils in each year group) allows primary English leaders to provide teachers and pupils with guidance and support in choosing quality, age-appropriate texts. This could take the form of a set list for each year group or a guide list for teachers to choose from. Some books from the reading spine may be included in English and reading lessons, while others may be read purely for enjoyment. In addition to the set list, leaving a few spaces for teachers to make their own choices with books they love or new books they discover is sure to increase the modelling of passionate sharing of treasured books. Asking teachers to identify their personal choices before sharing them with their classes will allow English leaders to check the appropriateness of what is being read and prevent duplication.

The books each school chooses to include in its reading spine will reflect the ethos and core values of the school. The inclusion of high-quality classics will build cultural capital, while careful selection of texts that celebrate diversity and build empathy will help children develop respect for others, care and self-confidence. Take time to identify these core values and consciously apply them when choosing books for children.

Schools should create their own reading spines with input from carefully curated external lists. This is a valuable conversation to have as a school team, making suggestions and discussing where to place each book. There may be differences of opinion. For example, should *The Lion, the Witch and the Wardrobe* be read aloud in Year 3, or should it be kept for a more independent read in Year 5? What's important is that children are given the chance to experience this essential text at some point on their primary school journey. It is up to their teachers to decide when and how.

When devising a reading spine, be sure to include:

- **classic stories** that are a part of literary tradition – these are stories and characters referred to in other books, on TV, in films and as a part of our day-to-day language, e.g. 'He's such a Scrooge'
- **contemporary books** that embrace diversity and real issues, develop empathy and take children on the most amazing adventures
- **poetry** that gives children opportunities to explore language and discover new ways to express themselves; this may include verse novels
- **non-fiction** that encourages children to ask questions about the world around them.

Support for creating a reading spine

There are many age-appropriate book lists available that can help inspire a reading spine.

Pie Corbett

Literacy expert Pie Corbett has created a read-aloud programme for Nursery to Year 6. This fantastic selection of books will give children a shared reference of stories and the opportunity to enjoy many books that have shaped generations of readers. It is a wonderful starting point for a school's own reading spine and can be easily updated with more recent must-read books.

What's brilliant about it isn't necessarily the list, but the idea: a common bank of stories allows pupils natural reference points to tap into during future reading, writing and discussion. It also lifts the burden of having to create this reading diet single-handed from the shoulders of class teachers. You can download the full list freely from the Reading Spine website (https://shop.scholastic.co.uk/reading-spine), together with tips for creating your own reading spine.

I'd use it as a foundation, rather than a definitive list. Some titles have been engrained as timeless classics for good reason; others will benefit from being read alongside newer books that better reflect the make-up of the children you teach.

Books for Topics

Books for Topics is an incredibly valuable resource. Its 50 Recommended Reads for each year group provides schools with core lists of classic and contemporary books to share with children. This wonderful blend of old and new addresses modern issues with inclusivity and celebrates many different people. The fiction, non-fiction and poetry recommendations are up to date, with short reviews giving additional insight into the content. See www.booksfortopics.com

Scott Evans: The Reader Teacher

Primary school teacher and reading expert Scott Evans has created an invaluable website, The Reader Teacher, for teachers (www.thereaderteacher.com). His Top 100 Recommended Reads for each year group is a fantastic starting point when devising a school reading spine. Each list has been carefully curated and his recommendations can be trusted.

Case study: The creation and curation of diverse reading spines

Christopher Harrison, headteacher, Oatlands Infant School

The creation of a whole-school reading spine needs to be done sensitively and collaboratively. Headteacher Christopher Harrison shares the underpinnings of his school's reading programme and the team's intentions as they create a reading journey for every child. This reading spine is a live document that is refined and curated as the school year progresses. There is space for new books, teacher choices and texts that respond to specific needs.

The Reading Framework 2022 includes a great section with key questions that educators should be asking about the books they provide in school, particularly those that they choose to have as focus / read-aloud texts. This provides a useful stepping-off point from which we can start to build our reading spines. From here, we can start to create our spines. I have always done this as a team via in-school CPD sessions. Ours is saved as a live document, so the whole team can curate it throughout the academic year. Most schools will have core topics mapped out, and pairing texts with these topics can have a real impact on children buying into their learning journey. For example, partnering a unit on explorers and journeys with Mostafa Salameh's biography and picture book creates real-world context that underpins the learning taking place. This grows pupils' cultural capital, while providing critical reference points throughout the unit. This in turn builds greater connections that lead to more deeply embedded learning.

We also need to consider the impact that incredible literature can have on people, particularly when it accurately shares and celebrates a range of cultures and communities. As you construct your spines, I would recommend pairing each text on the reading spine with a short 'heads up' statement. My preference would be to pre-read any book before sharing it with the pupils in my care. This isn't always possible, though, particularly if teachers are not avid readers, and this might lead to some complex and potentially upsetting conversations cropping up. For example, imagine if a pupil in your class had just lost a parent or carer; you would need to know that prior to reading Struan Murray's *Orphans of the Tide* or Sophie Anderson's *The House with Chicken Legs*. You'd need to know that Maz Evans' *Vi Spy* included fractured families if a pupil was going through that in your class, or that Ross Montgomery's *The Midnight Guardians* included a very intense section where bombs are dropped on London during the Blitz if you were reading to refugee children who had seen war. An example of this is on the following reading spine.

Category	Book / text	Heads up
WWII	*Owen and the Soldier* (Thompson)	Contains loss of immediate family, strong emotion
WWII	*When the Sky Falls* (Earle)	Contains loss of immediate family, scenes of bombing, strong emotion, dyslexic lead character
Vikings	*Odd and the Frost Giants* (Gaiman)	–
Vikings	*The Norse Myths* (Crossley-Holland)	–
WWII	*Now or Never: A Dunkirk Story* (Rai)	Contains loss of friends, references racist incidents
WWII	*After the War* (Palmer)	Contains loss of immediate family, references to Holocaust, strong emotion
Monsters and mayhem	*The Land of Roar* (McLachlan)	–

Category	Book / text	Heads up
Monsters and mayhem	*Dragonology* (Drake)	–
Journeys	*Journey to Jo'burg* (Naidoo)	Strong focus on Apartheid, references racist incidents including violence
Journeys	*The Arrival* (Tan)	Emotive / atmospheric illustrations that some pupils might find unnerving
The Amazon	*The Explorer* (Rundell)	–
The Amazon	*Journey to the River Sea* (Ibbotson)	–
The Amazon	*Wild World* (McAllister)	–
Space	*The Jamie Drake Equation* (Edge)	Parents working away from home
Space	*Hidden Figures* (Shetterly)	Reference to segregation, racism and sexism
Space	*Dr Maggie's Grand Tour of the Solar System* (Aderin-Pocock)	–
Maya	*Rain Player* (Wisniewski)	–
Maya	*Middleworld* (Voelkel)	–
Maya	*The Chocolate Tree: A Mayan Folktale* (Lowery and Keep)	–
Ancient Greece	*Who Let the Gods Out?* (Evans)	Reference to illness in family, includes early-onset Alzheimer's
Ancient Greece	*A Journey Through Greek Myths* (Ward and Berg)	–
Migration and refugees	*Boy, Everywhere* (Dassu)	–
Migration and refugees	*Boy 87* (Fountain)	–

Category	Book / text	Heads up
Looking to the future	*The Infinite* (Agbabi)	Neurodiverse main characters, strong references to climate change
Looking to the future	*A Trip to the Future* (Butterfield)	–
Primary–secondary transition	*Crater Lake* (Killick)	–
Primary–secondary transition	*The Humiliations of Welton Blake* (Wheatle)	–
Primary–secondary transition	*The Boy at the Back of the Class* (Raúf)	–

As a teacher, it is a privilege to witness the amazing moment when a child sees themselves in what they read or what is read to them. I have had pupils take home Ian Eagleton's *Nen and the Lonely Fisherman* to help them come out to their parents. I've had conversations with families of newly diagnosed autistic girls who see themselves reflected in Elle McNicoll's *A Kind of Spark* and *Show Us Who You Are*. I have seen dyslexic children connect with Joseph in Phil Earle's *When the Sky Falls*, and I have seen pupils with hearing impairments chuckling at Cece Bell's *El Deafo*. As a reader-teacher, nothing beats seeing a pupil's eyes light up as they see themselves reflected in the pages of the literature you have placed in front of them. Nothing beats a child seeing themselves reflected in the classroom and feeling valued, welcome and loved.

Further reading

Corbett, P., 'Reading Spine', https://shop.scholastic.co.uk/reading-spine

CHAPTER 9
MISCONCEPTIONS AND DIFFICULT CONCEPTS

Like me, I'm sure you'll have lost count of how many times you've marked writing tasks and discovered the same particular error occurring over and over again. For example, multiple pupils have written 'could of' in place of 'could have', because they have heard the contraction 'could've' and written down the sound. Patterns like this are not carelessness. They are misconceptions: things pupils have learned by ear and are applying consistently, but which do not hold up against how English is written.

The national curriculum for English describes precisely what primary pupils should know about phonics, spelling, grammar and punctuation (DfE, 2014). Much of teaching English is the work of teaching that knowledge and ensuring misconceptions don't stick. Some of them are caused by rules that pupils have only half learned. Some come from oddities embedded in the language itself – where there are just too many exceptions for rules to be trusted implicitly.

In 'Improving literacy in key stage 2', the Education Endowment Foundation recommends teachers plan activities that will reveal children's thinking and expose any gaps or misconceptions (EEF, 2021, p.39). In this chapter, I want to go one step further. As well as planning to diagnose misconceptions, we must also predict where they may occur in the future – and plan our teaching so they don't take root in the first place.

I've split the misconceptions I see most frequently into two categories: pupil misconceptions at word and sentence level, and adult misconceptions surrounding reading and vocabulary. I've left detailed strategies for tackling them until the end of the chapter – first, because the list is long; second, because the strategies will make more sense if you know what problems they're aiming to solve.

Misconceptions for children

At word level

The teaching of phonics develops children's knowledge and understanding of the relationship between written symbols and sounds. In younger children, this approach can have a really positive impact (5+ months' progress), especially when embedded in a rich literacy environment as one part of a successful literacy strategy (EEF, 2025).

When older pupils struggle with reading and spelling, it's important to identify exactly what is causing difficulty. If it's decoding, phonics could still be an effective approach. Identify gaps in their phonetic understanding and provide bespoke teaching to address the need. However, if they have been exposed to phonics teaching for a number of years and are still not retaining it, there may be other issues that need to be investigated, such as dyslexia, memory or processing.

Over-reliance on spelling rules

Most of us were taught 'i before e, except after c' at some point. Very few of us were taught how quickly that rule falls apart. Try it against weird, neighbour and conscience, and the pattern is already gone.

I find it more useful to treat rules of this kind as a starting point rather than a resting place. Give the children the rule, then set them a sorting task with conforming words in one column and exceptions in another, and ask them what the exception words might have in common. Etymology (the study of the origin of words) is a rich seam here. If a class becomes curious about why conscience is spelled the way it is, that curiosity does most of the teaching for you. Over time, children who have studied words in this way develop a visual sense of correct spelling that a memorised rule does not produce on its own.

Reading widely supports the same outcome. The more often a child meets these spellings in print, the more settled the correct form becomes.

Spelling common exception words

Common exception words (also known as high-frequency words) occur often in texts. They may be as simple as 'the' or 'have', or as complex as 'receive' or 'recommend'. These types of words are also called 'sight words', as children are often taught to recognise them at a glance without needing to decode. A number of sight words do not follow regular phonetic spelling patterns, which is what makes them more difficult to remember. Add to this that many of these words, especially in younger year groups, do not have an easily definable meaning (for example 'to' or 'is') and you have the perfect recipe for common spelling errors.

When it comes to learning common exception words, regular exposure is the answer: play memory games, display a small group of words, spot them while reading, investigate parts of a word and talk about why they are spelled that way.

Avoid calling these words 'tricky words'. Any negative connotation with spelling can only put children off and limit self-confidence.

Using a / an correctly

This misconception often lies in the belief that 'a' precedes any noun beginning with a consonant while 'an' precedes any noun beginning with a vowel. It is not the letter but the sound that determines which article is used. For example, 'an hour', 'a house', 'a uniform' and 'an uncle' are all correct.

Using apostrophes correctly

Possession

Take time to explore the use of apostrophes to show ownership. Often, singular nouns are quite straightforward, but plural nouns, including irregular plurals like 'children', tend to be more difficult. Providing many examples allows children to see the words written correctly and then use them in their own writing. When it comes to using an apostrophe with words that already end with 's', there is no one set rule. Decide as a school how to teach it and stick with that. For example, the book belonging to Thomas may be Thomas's book or Thomas' book.

Contraction

Using an apostrophe to shorten two words into one takes practice. Give a clear explanation of which letters the apostrophe is replacing and plenty of time for children to do it themselves. Be sure to introduce more irregular contractions such as 'won't' and 'shan't'.

Its and it's

'Its' and 'it's' are often used incorrectly, as they don't follow the typical apostrophe for possession rule. Link 'its' with 'his' and 'hers', while 'it's' goes with 'he's' (he is) and 'she's' (she is).

Understanding homophones and homonyms

Homophones are pairs (or more) of words that sound the same when spoken but have both a different meaning and a different spelling (for example there / their / they're, blue / blew, write / right).

Homonyms are pairs of words that have the same spelling but have different meanings and may also have different pronunciations (for example orange, glasses, bark, read).

With both homophones and homonyms, it is important to spend time exploring the words and their meanings. Play games, use the words orally, use them in sentences and revisit them often.

Believing all adverbs end in 'ly'

When pupils are first adding more description to their writing, it can be easy to ask them to show how a character is doing something by adding an 'ly word' – an adverb. The problem occurs when children hang on to that as the definition of an adverb and do not extend their understanding to include other words that show how (manner), as well as adverbs of time, place and frequency.

At sentence level

Use of capital letters and full stops

The misuse of capital letters is something that plagues teachers of all year groups. Using them correctly at the beginning of sentences, along with full stops at the end, directly links to a basic understanding of sentence structure. Revisit the components of a simple sentence, emphasising that it is not complete without the capital letter (and end punctuation).

Children will often use a capital letter to begin their own name and those of their friends because that is how they have always seen them printed. Build on this by talking about the difference between common and proper nouns. Ensure all text in the classroom follows the rules for capitalisation (for example, use lowercase letters on lists of common nouns).

Sentence construction

Modelling and encouraging children to speak in full sentences is key to helping them write in complete sentences. If children are writing in fragments rather than full sentences, spend time revisiting the definition of a simple sentence (one subject + one verb). Only once this is secure will they be able to manipulate these independent clauses into compound and complex sentences.

A comma splice occurs when a writer uses a comma to separate two independent (main) clauses in a sentence. In this case, a comma is not strong enough. Instead, a full stop (to create two simple sentences), a semi-colon or a conjunction (to create a complex sentence) is required. To spot a comma splice, children need to be secure in the difference between a main / subordinate clause (complete / incomplete or independent / dependent).

Sometimes children get so caught up in what they're writing that sentences run on and on. These sentences may be technically correct, with conjunctions and punctuation joining the clauses, but they're exhausting for the reader and soon lose sense. Encourage children to add punctuation to break up a run-on sentence into shorter parts.

Use of commas

Whether it's in a list, after an opening adverbial phrase (fronted adverbial), following a subordinate clause at the beginning of a sentence or to embed a clause in the middle of a sentence, commas can be one of the most difficult types of punctuation for children to get right. This is where modelling is key. Children need to see commas used correctly so they can imitate the rules in their own writing. Point them out in real books, and allow pupils time to practise using them in their own sentences.

Punctuating speech

Help children understand how to punctuate speech correctly by pointing it out in the books they read, correctly modelling it often and giving them many opportunities to practise. This is a lesson that needs to be revisited regularly. One of the most difficult concepts is knowing where to put the end punctuation. Is it a full stop or a comma? Is it inside or outside the final inverted commas? Take time to explain the rules.

Misconceptions for adults

Children are not the only ones to hold misconceptions in primary English. Some of the most persistent misconceptions are those held by teachers and schools, and they are worth naming because they shape how reading and vocabulary are taught across the curriculum.

Reading misconceptions

Reading once is enough

Rereading a text builds fluency in the reader. It also gives children the opportunity to increase accuracy of word identification, their reading speed and expression. Greater fluency then leads to greater comprehension.

Adults can make the error of assuming children need to read a text only once because their own comprehension as an adult is secure after one reading. Children who do not have the same degree of fluency may need to reread a text multiple times to find the same level of meaning.

This rereading should not occur all in one sitting. Revisit the text over several days, allowing children to experience it with greater understanding and fluency each time. For example:

- Day one – Teacher and children read together. Follow along. Model fluent reading.
- Day two – Children read aloud. Activate background knowledge. Answer questions.
- Day three – Children read independently. Further discussion and questions. Make connections with other texts, their own life and their knowledge of the world.

Adapted from Reading Strategies and Misconceptions website (see 'Further reading')

Being able to answer questions about a passage equals good comprehension

There is so much more to reading comprehension than simple retrieval. Pulling basic facts from a text is a start, but it does not tell a teacher just how much a pupil has understood. Further discussion and follow-up questions allow children to think more deeply about what they have read and formulate their own questions. Encourage them to make connections to what they already know by using strategies to activate their background knowledge. Build in opportunities for inference, analyse the author's use of language, make comparisons and consider how the text has been sequenced and structured to enhance meaning.

Pupils who can read fluently have strong comprehension

The Simple View of Reading, a model first proposed by Gough and Tunmer (1986), shows that reading is made up of two components: word reading (decoding) and language comprehension. It is when both of these elements come together that children become successful readers. Fluency alone does not mean a child has understood what they have read. Children may have good word reading skills but poor language comprehension. Teachers need to give children plenty of opportunities to talk about what they have read, both to assess and develop their comprehension.

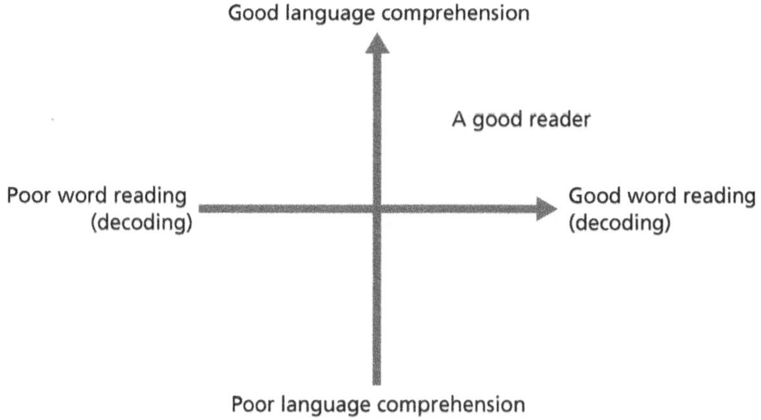

▲ **Figure 9.1 The simple view of reading**

Vocabulary misconceptions

Knowing the definition of the word is enough

There is so much more to developing a strong vocabulary than just understanding the meaning of words (semantics). The multiple dimensions of word learning also include morphology (the structure or parts of the word), pronunciation, the grammar and classification of the word, etymology (word origin) and spelling. Giving children opportunities to explore a word, use it orally and link it to their prior knowledge ensures they have a rich understanding, and will be able to remember and use the word when they meet it again in the future.

Weekly vocabulary lists are effective

When a list of words is assigned completely out of context and children are asked to write the definition or use each word in a sentence, they may struggle to make connections to their own knowledge or other areas of learning. As a result, children are unlikely to be fully engaged in word learning and the list is easily forgotten. It is far more effective to learn new words through reading aloud to children and exploring vocabulary together, or linking vocabulary development to class topics. Context is key.

It is possible to pre-teach all the difficult words in a text

When preparing to use a new text, it is essential that teachers consider the vocabulary children will encounter. Some words may already be familiar to the children, while others will be new. It is not important to teach every new word they come across but, instead, focus on the tier two vocabulary. These are words they are likely to encounter again in another context and will serve them in the future. Subject-specific tier three vocabulary should be touched on when reading, encouraging children to use context clues and knowledge of morphology (the structure or parts of the word) to work out what it might mean (Rasinski and Padak, 2012).

Strategies for addressing and avoiding misconceptions

Having named the misconceptions, I want to turn to how to prevent and address them. Most of the following approaches apply across the word-level, sentence-level and adult-facing misconceptions above.

Anticipate, don't just react

Experienced teaching of English depends heavily on anticipation. Before a lesson, ask yourself where children are likely to go wrong with the specific concept being taught. If teaching apostrophes of contraction, you might predict that some children will put the apostrophe in the wrong position within the contracted word. Plan a specific opportunity to catch it. After the lesson, reflect on which misconceptions actually surfaced and what caused them, then carry those notes into the next planning cycle.

Model explicitly

When teaching a concept for the first time, show it being done. Explain what you are doing as you do it, and be explicit about the decisions you are making (why that apostrophe, why that comma). The clearer the model, the less room there is for a misconception to form from guesswork.

Build a bank of examples, and use non-examples

Children need to see a range of examples of a concept done correctly before they can produce their own. As their confidence grows, push the examples outwards into harder cases. Non-examples are equally useful. Give pupils sentences containing mistakes and ask them to spot and correct them: children take genuine delight in explaining why the teacher has got it wrong. Both sorting (correct and incorrect examples) and repair tasks sharpen their attention to the rule being tested.

Embed grammar in reading and writing

Grammar taught in isolation is easily forgotten. Grammar pointed out in the middle of a text the class is already reading, or tested in the middle of a piece of writing the child cares about, tends to stay. Look for chances to point out real examples of grammar objectives as they appear, and challenge children to use them in the writing they are already doing.

Rules and definitions: keep them few and clear

Give precise definitions or rules that children can refer back to, but do not overwhelm the lesson with too many of them at once. Always make sure children understand the reasoning behind a rule rather than relying on the rule itself, because English has exceptions to nearly every rule worth teaching. Help children notice the exceptions and discuss why they might exist.

Watch for early signs

When teaching a concept you know tends to be difficult, watch closely for children who are already showing signs of misunderstanding in the early part of the lesson. Nip it in the bud with verbal feedback and another example. Do not be afraid to stop the class and revisit a point to make sure everyone is with you.

Repeat and revisit

Difficult concepts need to be returned to often. A single lesson on comma splices will not do the work. Build in opportunities to revisit the concept over several weeks, in varied contexts, until correct use becomes automatic.

Use immediate feedback

Immediate feedback while a lesson is still in progress is the most powerful tool you have for dealing with misconceptions. React to what is happening in the room and adjust your teaching accordingly rather than waiting to pick up the mistakes in marking.

Looking ahead

The next chapter, on assessment, turns from preventing and addressing misconceptions to judging what children have learned. Many of the assessment strategies it discusses draw directly on the same principles as this chapter: uncover what children are actually thinking and plan your next teaching step from there.

Further reading

Gough, P.B. and Tunmer, W.E. (1986) 'Decoding, reading and reading disability'. *Remedial and Special Education*, 7(1), 6–10.

Misconceptions, Reading strategies and misconceptions, https://readingstrategiesmsu.weebly.com/misconceptions.html

CHAPTER 10
ASSESSMENT IN PRIMARY ENGLISH

When I listen to a child read aloud or look over their shoulder at a draft, I am assessing. Most of this work never produces a score or appears in a spreadsheet. It tells me what a pupil can do now and what they still find difficult, which is what shapes my planning for next week.

This is the kind of assessment that does most of the work in day-to-day English teaching. The UKLA puts the point plainly: assessment should not 'only (or always) be "high stakes"'; it should 'primarily be to understand what students know and can do in order to support their future learning' ('UKLA Viewpoints: Assessing English'). Statutory tests and end-of-key-stage judgements matter as well, and I come to those later in the chapter. Most of this book's focus, though, is on the assessment that happens in small, informal moments across a week of lessons.

Assessment is an essential component of the teaching and learning cycle (Figure 10.1). It allows teachers to determine how much pupils understand and the success of previous lessons. It stimulates reflection and analysis and informs future planning.

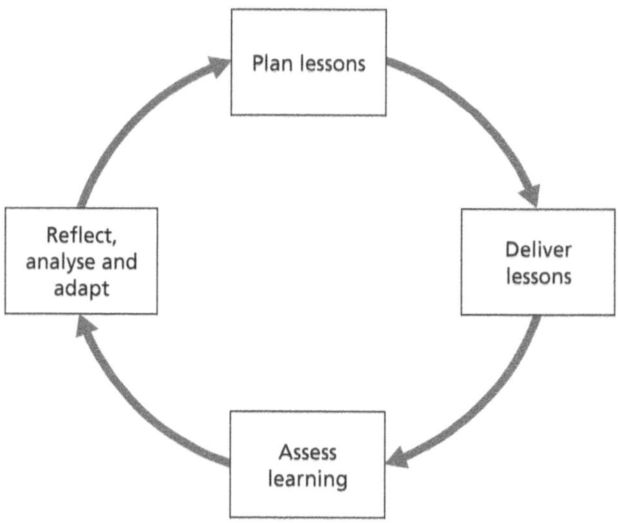

▲ **Figure 10.1 Assessment is an essential component of the teaching and learning cycle**

Assessment is not testing for the sake of finding out what 'level' pupils are working at or to submit data. It is a balance of formative and summative strategies for the purpose of informing teaching and helping children to learn as much as possible. In primary, this assessment also includes preparation for statutory assessment. Teachers, especially in Year 6, must walk the fine line of supporting children to do the best they can in their end-of-key-stage tests without continually teaching to the test and overwhelming the class with past papers.

Formative assessment

Assessment is so much more than an end-of-topic test or spelling quiz. Quality formative assessment allows teachers to continually find out what pupils understand (and don't understand), enabling them to adjust their teaching accordingly. This may be from one lesson to the next or mid-lesson as misconceptions arise, and the plan needs to shift to meet the needs of the pupils. Using formative assessment effectively takes confidence and a willingness to stray from the plan. When opportunities to assess are regular, focused and intentionally planned, teachers are able to respond to their pupils and the overall experience is much more effective.

Within active and adaptive teaching, formative assessment is assessment *for* learning. It helps teachers ensure pupils are on the right track and are understanding and retaining the intended objectives. In his keynote address at the Cambridge Assessment Network Conference in 2006, Dylan Wiliam compared formative assessment to a pilot flying a plane. Throughout the journey, the pilot is taking constant readings and making careful adjustments in response to wind, currents and weather. At the end of the journey, the plane should be where the pilot intended it to be. In the same way, teachers take readings of pupils' understanding and progress then make careful adjustments to meet their needs. At the end of the lesson or series of lessons, the pupils should achieve the objectives the teachers originally set out for them (Wiliam, 2006).

By asking themselves the following questions, teachers can make clear decisions about assessment for learning:

- Where are the pupils now?
- Where are pupils going?
- How are we going to get there?
- What regular progress checks can I make along the way?

Dylan Wiliam suggests five key strategies for assessment for learning. These will help teachers develop formative assessment techniques that are not gimmicky, token or just skimming the surface, but are meaningful and provide real information.

1 Clarify and understand learning intentions and criteria for success.
2 Engineer effective classroom discussions, questions and tasks that elicit evidence of learning.
3 Provide feedback that moves pupils forwards.
4 Activate pupils as instructional resources for each other.
5 Activate pupils as owners of their own learning.

Summative assessment

Summative assessment measures what pupils have learned at a specific point in time. This is assessment *of* learning and often takes place at the end of a teaching unit, half-term, term or year. It is used to assess achievement, provide data for analysis at the class, school, local authority / trust and national level, and to report to parents.

Summative assessment helps teachers determine whether pupils are working at, below or above age or year-group expectations. As such, it is important these assessments are standardised across the group being assessed and are moderated where appropriate. In some cases, such as key stage 2 SATs, summative assessments are marked externally and only the results are reported back to school.

Gone are the days of levelling using APP (Assessing Pupil Progress) sheets and finding the best fit among the descriptors. Many schools now have some form of central progression grids that allow teachers to track pupils' achievement of a series of objectives. A formula will then determine whether a pupil is working below, at or above the required standard. Formative assessments may help to inform these judgements, as well as summative tests and independent writing activities. These assessment grids may be school made or a bought-in resource. However they are created, it's essential to consider teacher workload and the number of data drops required each year. Find a balance between gathering important information and allowing teachers to get on and teach rather than spending time testing.

Children working significantly below age-related expectations may be assessed using a separate system, such as PIVATS for SEND (Sensible

Senco, 2026). Teachers will receive information on the system that should be used from their school SENDCO or an external agency supporting the school.

Moderation

Moderation of summative assessment judgements is a positive and supportive way of making sure everyone is on the same page. Teachers are able to discuss what pupils have achieved and also identify targets that will help them move forwards. During moderation sessions, it's essential that everyone is working from the same, clear marking criteria. Having a common language allows teachers, senior leaders and the local authority / trust to discuss pupils' reading or writing effectively.

Moderation sessions are often offered by the local authority for teachers in statutory assessment year groups. These sessions help teachers understand national expectations, with the aim of more consistent judgements across the country. Moderation within school is even more valuable, as it allows everyone, including teachers not currently working in statutory assessment years, to understand national expectations. These sessions may take place within year-group teams, within the same key stage or across key stages. Building this common language, expectation and consistency is powerful professional development for all teachers.

Diagnostic assessment

A third type of assessment is diagnostic assessment. This assessment *about* learning is particularly important in primary English, as teachers identify pupils who may require extra support, gaps in understanding or areas of the curriculum that need further attention.

Diagnostic assessment may take place at the beginning of a unit of work – before any teaching takes place – to help teachers plan the most appropriate learning journey. Identifying what children already know, and don't know, avoids wasting time on areas where they are already secure, and shines a light on where more attention is required.

Diagnostic assessment may also be used to identify areas of difficulty, such as reading or writing speed, gaps in phonics knowledge, the ability to write using specific features or spelling misconceptions. As well as informing future teaching, this can help identify children who would benefit from targeted interventions.

Marking and feedback

Carefully considered, meaningful feedback can have a huge impact on children's progress. The Education Endowment Foundation has found that feedback can have an impact of +6 months' progress, while verbal feedback – the most effective – can have an impact of +7 months (EEF, b).

▼ **Table 10.1 Effective feedback**

Who?	Feedback may be provided by peers, teachers and other adults in the classroom, or even by technology.
When?	Feedback may be given during, immediately after or some time after learning. The sooner feedback is given, the more impact it will have.
What?	The most valuable feedback gives specific information on how to improve. Children benefit from hearing about what is correct, as well as what is incorrect. Feedback may be given about the task, the subject content or self-regulation strategies (the ability of children to manage their own behaviour and aspects of their learning) (EEF, a).
How?	Feedback may be written or given verbally, one to one, in small groups or to the whole class. Whole-class feedback sheets may be created to share with the class, highlighting key successes and common misconceptions / areas for development.

Primary English is always at risk of a heavy workload when it comes to feedback and marking. It is important that school leaders are mindful of this when establishing policies and expectations around the amount of written feedback required.

Verbal feedback

As verbal feedback has been shown to have a greater impact on pupil progress than written feedback, and it reduces teacher workload, it's clearly a strategy worth building into the school day. Live marking and verbal feedback prevent misconceptions from becoming embedded (Early Career Hub, 2020). Children are able to respond to positives and corrections on the spot without having to remember what they've written (sometimes days previously) and without the ability to read any written comments.

When giving verbal feedback, teachers should make effective use of questioning, prompt pupils to elaborate and explain their thinking and help pupils to clarify their learning goals. The more teachers and children practise giving and receiving verbal feedback, the easier and more effective it will become.

By making feedback a part of the lesson, teachers are able to stop pupils and address common misconceptions right away. They may choose to teach a mini-lesson about one part of the success criteria or quickly review a concept from the main teaching. This is the perfect time to grab the book of a child who is doing well and showcase it using a visualiser. Ask children to identify examples of the lesson objective. Once the particular focus has been addressed, pupils can carry on working.

Written feedback

When written feedback is being used, it's important to give children something to action in their response. This could be correcting spellings, improving punctuation or reworking a specific sentence or paragraph. Be sure to plan in time for children to do this properly without rushing.

Many schools use a series of marking symbols to help children spot where they have made a spelling error, missed a full stop or capital letter or made some other small error. This list of symbols should be consistent across school. There may be a simpler version for key stage 1, with additional symbols used in key stage 2, but using familiar symbols as children move through school will speed up their response time and aid understanding for everyone.

Time spent marking books can be greatly reduced by getting the children involved first. Plan marking and feedback time into lessons and develop a culture of working hard to spot successes and areas for improvement. Children can comment (verbally or in writing) about what went well and things to improve. Encourage them to highlight places where they've met the success criteria or star areas where they were a bit stuck. They could draw a box around an area they would particularly like feedback on (MacNeill). Thinking about their learning and how they've achieved is empowering for children and helps them retain what they've learned.

Peer assessment

Effective peer assessment needs to be taught with clear routines and expectations. It's important that children retain ownership of their own work and no one else writes on it. Feedback from peers can be very helpful, but it's always up to the child whether or not they choose to take their peer's advice.

In a peer feedback session, a child may read their writing to their partner (or have it read aloud by an adult). The partner offers verbal advice linked to success criteria. Teachers may wish to provide a bank of feedback phrases for children to use as they learn to give clear, constructive feedback (MacNeill, '5 ways to improve feedback in primary school').

Assessment strategies

Spoken language – formative assessment:

- Assessment and feedback of ongoing day-to-day spoken language (adult:child and child:child)
- Adult responses with appropriate modelling
- Encouraging and modelling appropriate vocabulary
- Document evidence on sticky notes, in a notebook or on a computer file (stand-out moments, achievements, signs of progress)
- Adapt teaching based on interactions with children.

Spoken language – summative assessment:

- Go through notes and make judgements about the attainment of objectives on the school's spoken-language progression grid.
- Use teacher-held knowledge to inform judgements.
- Reflect on next steps for that child.
- Identify areas to focus on with the class – either because objectives have not yet been taught or children need more practice and opportunity.

Reading – formative assessment:

- Give immediate feedback during phonics and reading lessons.
- Listen to children read aloud and give them opportunities to talk about what they're reading.
- Watch and listen for misconceptions, and whether or not children are able to resolve them.
- Pay attention to responses and comments during reading lessons. Look for instances where children are making use of background knowledge or finding evidence to back up their responses.
- Make notes of evidence from discussion.
- Give verbal feedback encouraging children to think again or extend their responses.
- Consider written responses in English / reading books.

Reading – summative assessment:

- Use running records to assess decoding ability.
- Track progress on book bands.
- Review comments in home reading records or reading journals.
- Give independent comprehension checks orally or written.
- Use past papers sparingly to help children become familiar with the format / timing and to check scaled scores in the run-up to key stage 2 SATs.
- Use reading age tests.
- Use online programmes such as Accelerated Reader to gain insight into pupils' quiz results.
- Use a range of evidence to make judgements about the attainment of objectives on the school reading progression grid.
- In Year 2, use the Teacher Assessment Framework (DfE, 2017) to assess whether children have achieved all the statement for 'Working towards the expected standard', 'Working at the expected standard' or 'Working at greater depth'.
- Reflect on what needs to be addressed to help children continue to make progress.
- Moderate judgements with colleagues.

Writing – formative assessment:

- Provide live marking and immediate feedback as children are planning and drafting.
- Work with children 1:1 or in small groups to address misconceptions, work towards targets and discuss next steps.
- Provide purposeful, written comments that children can read and action.
- Hold half-termly or termly writing conferences with children to discuss their successes and areas for development.

Writing – summative assessment:

- Assess spelling in a variety of ways, including short tests.
- Assess grammar and punctuation through written work and short tests.
- Provide opportunities for independent writing.

- Use a range of evidence from all stages of the writing process, including writing from across the curriculum, to make judgements about the attainment of objectives on the school writing-progression grid.
- In Year 2 and Year 6, use the Teacher Assessment Framework (DfE, 2017) to assess whether children have achieved all the statements for 'Working towards the expected standard', 'Working at the expected standard' or 'Working at greater depth'.
- Moderate judgements with colleagues.

Attainment versus progress

Attainment is the academic standard a child reaches at a particular point in time. This might be the score they achieve on a specific test, or an overall description of working at, above or below the expected standard. Attainment is usually recorded as a grade, score or level, and is a key measure at the end of each key stage.

Progress is a measure of how a child improves over time. It considers their prior and current attainment to show difference over time. This may be from the beginning of the school year to the end, or from the end of key stage 1 to the end of key stage 2.

Progress is never completely linear. Children make progress in English at different rates, with accelerations, pauses and even what appears to be going backwards at times. This is all a part of their development as they consolidate learning and get ready for next steps. Progress is affected by a number of factors, including quality of teaching, classroom environment and attitude to learning, as well social and emotional factors. Teachers need to be mindful of vulnerable children (looked after, pupil premium, SEND) to ensure other factors in their lives do not have a negative effect on progress and, ultimately, attainment.

Teachers can work to accelerate children's progress through quality-first teaching, carefully planned assessment for learning, intentional adaptive teaching as required and targeted interventions.

Strategies for accelerating progress

The Learning by Questions Hub suggests seven strategies for accelerating progress (Learning by Questions, 2023):

1 **Retrieval practice:** Giving children opportunities to consolidate their learning in previous topics ensures they have a firm foundation on

which to place the next blocks of learning. Retrieval practice helps them remember key information as they revisit previous topics and make links to new learning.

2 **Scaffold content when introducing new topics:** Scaffolding involves breaking up the learning into sections and providing a tool, or structure, with each section (Alber, 2011). This scaffolding gives every child the support they need to access the learning.

3 **Focused practice:** Focused practice builds confidence in pupils. Using drills to solidify knowledge of something like spellings can work well for some children. It is one of many strategies to include in the teaching of concepts that need to be memorised.

4 **Effective marking:** Use meaningful, manageable and motivating written feedback to help children make progress. This does not mean every piece of work should have extensive written comments. Use agreed symbols and challenge questions to encourage children to think about their learning in a new way.

5 **Appropriate, relevant and directive feedback:** Whether verbal or written, aim to provide specific feedback for children. Ask further questions, guide children to spot misconceptions and provide opportunities for children to respond and improve their work.

6 **Identify gaps in learning:** Using diagnostic assessments and question-level analysis helps teachers identify common misconceptions and areas of difficulty for specific children. Use this information to inform next steps.

7 **Intervention:** Targeted interventions give teachers opportunities to address very specific areas of learning with small groups of children. These interventions should be focused and time limited. The member of staff leading the intervention should be clear on the intended outcomes, and use strategies that will keep children on-task and help them to remember their new learning.

Further reading

Alber, R. (2011) '6 Scaffolding Strategies to Use With Your Students'. Edutopia, www.edutopia.org/blog/scaffolding-lessons-six-strategies-rebecca-alber

UKLA Viewpoints: Assessing English, https://ukla.org/ukla_resources/ukla-viewpoints-assessing-english/

CHAPTER 11
LINKS WITH OTHER SUBJECTS

As a Year 4 class are reading *The Iron Man*, they may study character and setting as part of their English lessons; while, in art, they might use the story as inspiration for a scrap-metal sculpture. The English lesson doesn't suddenly become an art lesson, or vice versa, but having that shared text at the centre gives the children a reason to write or make something they truly care about.

This is why I'm inclined to agree with Gareth Pimley, who believes good primary school practice should encompass both rigorous discrete subject teaching and effective cross-curricular links, as strong subject knowledge creates a foundation that can be built upon (Pimley, 2011). Cross-curricular teaching is not a replacement for subject lessons. When done well, it allows children to encounter again – and properly deploy – the language and ideas they have learned in class.

Cross-curricular, or topic, learning is simply an approach to structuring the curriculum where subjects are taught together in a themed way, as opposed to discrete, stand-alone lessons. After all, learning hardly ever occurs in isolation, particularly in the primary classroom. Many children are motivated by a well-planned topic and parents often find it easier to follow up theme learning at home – from reading books related to the topic to doing experiments or visiting museums together.

It's important to consider that not all pupils come to school with extensive background knowledge about what they read and learn. This is where cross-curricular activities become incredibly valuable. Teachers are able to help pupils develop essential content knowledge that will support reading comprehension and further learning.

The risk, worth flagging early, is of becoming so focused on the theme that essential skills and objectives are missed. Don't make links for the sake of it. The rest of this chapter sets out the subject-by-subject ideas I have found work well, and the kind of thinking that helps a teacher decide when a link is genuinely worth pursuing.

Planning cross-curricular links

Creating a concept map

When it comes to topic learning, I have found it useful to begin with a concept map. Write your potential theme in the centre of the page and create branches with the different subject areas around it. Select one or two subjects to act as the main hosts of the theme / topic (history and English for Ancient Greeks, for example), and allow yourself some brainstorming time to jot down possible links and activities across the curriculum areas, keeping in mind the knowledge and skills that need to be covered in each subject. Follow only those paths that allow both sides to do meaningful work. Once you have mapped out which links are worthy of being explored, you can plan out a sequence of lessons across your unit, ensuring you cover topics in such a way that the children are hitting objectives for each subject in every lesson, as well as making connections through their learning.

Mark Beales, writing on Cambridge University's education blog, has compiled a helpful list of principles for this type of planning (Beales, 2019). The take-home points I would emphasise are simple: consider the curriculum as one interconnected document rather than planning subject by subject; hook into calendar events such as Remembrance Day or World Book Day when planning themes; plan with other subject leads, not in isolation; utilise the language children have at home. Finally, don't force links that aren't there.

Links with other subjects

PSHE

English and PSHE support each other well as PSHE lessons are almost always communicative. Two aspects repay most of the planning time spent integrating them. First is reading for empathy, which Chapter 2 explores further. Whether it's through a novel or a picture book, children can be given opportunities to sit with situations different from their own. PSHE lessons then develop what the reading initiates. Using Onjali Q. Raúf's *The Boy at the Back of the Class* as a shared reader leaves you with a Year 5 class full of discussion points about refugees and what friendship looks like in difficult situations.

Second is persuasive and discursive writing about issues that matter to children. Asking pupils to write a letter to the headteacher setting out reasons for changing break-time routines, or drafting a speech taking a stance on one of your local council's decisions, helps them learn how to structure arguments in a context that values their opinions. When PSHE drives the learning, English contributes through writing. Child-led talk comes first. Circle discussion and more structured debate both hone the thinking children can bring to their next piece of written argument, and ending a PSHE lesson with a short piece of written reflection can be an extremely effective link back to English writing.

History

Every history topic has a seam of attached texts: myths, folk tales, biographies and historical accounts. Most writing done well in a history lesson is doing English work at the same time.

In my experience, when teaching a historical period, the strongest connections are made by drawing on its voices and genres. Year 3 pupils studying Ancient Greece don't just learn facts about early human society, they read myths and legends about fascinating gods and goddesses and then write their own, modelling their creations on the structures of traditional tales. Year 5 children learning about the Victorians might create a newspaper front-page report on the opening of the Great Exhibition. In both examples, the writing is anchored by historical content but also deepens pupils' understanding as they have to empathise with the period.

When you are using history as the host subject, English does its job via vocabulary and oracy. Children learn period-specific vocabulary (monarch, settlement, invasion, revolution) and develop their understanding of causation by arguing about it verbally. Stuart Tiffany, author of the excellent book, *Mr T Does Primary History*, which is worth consulting when planning linked lessons across the curriculum, says watching a good history lesson unfold 'looks a lot like a reading comprehension but it's not, children are learning to weigh evidence not look for the correct answer' (Tiffany, 2023). Discussion, drama and role play are useful in both subjects for this reason.

Religious education

RE in primary schools requires pupils to consider and evaluate traditions that may be very different from their own. Since that work depends on texts that are both sacred and traditional, it requires pupils to read carefully for both meaning and tone; in this way, it overlaps with English to an extent that makes joint planning straightforward.

When English is the host subject, the natural links are with traditional tales. Creation stories from across the religions, studied side by side as part of a unit on myths and origins, provide children with rich opportunities for comparison. Writing a recount of a visit to a place of worship also fits easily in English. The recount genre demands that children attend carefully to what they saw and describe it using a register appropriate to the setting.

When RE is the host subject, English works best when it provides children with a structure for their talking and their writing. Listening to a visitor from a faith community and then writing a thank-you letter to them demands focus from children; they have to decide what was most memorable. Writing a short response that compares two religious texts asks children to use the same technical language that they would when comparing two poems. The national curriculum doesn't dictate content for RE (this is covered by locally agreed syllabuses), but the English skills required by RE sit comfortably within the programme of study.

Geography

Geography and English both involve the concept of place, and both depend on noticing. It's rare to find a geography lesson that doesn't have a text in it somewhere, and a good English lesson studying a text set in any real or imagined place will draw on geographical knowledge.

If English is the host subject, something as simple as a class-read book can do a lot of the work for you. Putting up a world map and adding pins to mark the settings of books you've read over the course of the year gives pupils a visual record of where their books have taken them. Migration stories are another obvious choice, offering a window into topics of movement and belonging.

If geography is the host subject, the strongest English connections will ask pupils to describe and explain. Asking them to write a short explanation of how volcanoes erupt or describing the features on a journey walked as a class will give children purpose for remembering the technical vocabulary they have learned in your lessons. Ben Ballin, writing for *Leading Primary Geography*, argues that we should look for 'meaningful overlaps': places where teaching one thing strengthens teaching another (Ballin, 2019).

Science

Science is fundamentally about observing and explaining. It goes hand in hand with English. Explanation and observation are two types of writing that recur again and again in cross-curricular science lessons. Pupils writing about how a plant absorbs water or what goes on inside a volcano have something tangible to gain from using subject-specific vocabulary and from organising their writing so that the reader can follow their explanation, step by step. Keeping a notebook over a half-term or writing a poem about a patch of ground from one season to the next encourages children to slow down and look closely at the world around them. The right picture book can provide a doorway into either of those activities.

Science lessons can also give more purpose to writing in English. Investigation reports provide a real-life context for the use of causal conjunctions and subject-specific vocabulary. Having to record results encourages children to think about their reader, who wasn't there to see and experience what they did. Writing about the lives of scientists allows pupils to see curiosity in action, and it gives English teachers an opportunity to ensure that pupils read widely in non-fiction. For a more in-depth look at how to map progression in writing against progression in scientific knowledge at school age, read Jane Andrews and Charlotte Jackson's article for *Herts for Learning* (Andrews and Jackson, 2018).

Maths

Maths is the subject where cross-curricular work with English needs most finesse. Many suggestions trotted out for this ('write a story about a triangle'; 'keep a maths journal') are shown, on closer inspection, to be exercises in English dressed in pseudo-maths clothing. They teach children about English and little that is genuinely mathematical. Remember that golden thread running through this chapter? Only make meaningful links.

Here are two possibilities. The first is picture books with mathematical content that is integral to the story rather than mere window dressing. *The Perfect Fit*, by Naomi Jones and James Jones, has geometry driving its narrative, for example, so reading it is an act of mathematical thinking as much as literacy. Kerry Dalton's article about cross-curricular maths on the Third Space Learning blog has loads more examples (Dalton, 2026). The other is getting children to write about their mathematical thinking. When you ask pupils to write about a mistake they made tackling a problem, and how they spotted and corrected it, or to explain in their own words why a method works, you force them to put the precision that maths demands onto the page. It is harder than most writing because it demands clarity of logical order rather than narrative flow.

When maths is the host subject, less is more – for example, a sentence describing the most important thing pupils learned that week. Short summaries are better than longer written responses, which risk losing the mathematical thread.

Computing

Computing easily partners with English at the level of tools: the computing devices and software pupils use for English are also the easiest publishing tools for their writing. But there are stronger connections than 'type my story in Word', and the best ones relate to how computing can help pupils think about sequence and precision.

When English is the main subject, presentation and programming tie in best. Making a multimedia version of a finished piece of writing (a stop-motion animation of a narrative poem; a green-screen news report of a historical event) gives pupils an audience beyond the teacher and a reason to edit towards performance. Writing an email to a child in another school, or to an author whose books you've been reading, can give your class a purpose for drafting, and a real audience for the finished work.

When computing is the lead subject, English comes into play with explanation and debugging. Explaining, step by step, what a program does and why it went wrong is as demanding an explanatory text as anything they'll write in science. The language is the same too: *first, next, because, unless, until*. Writing in this way makes children more precise writers across all subjects.

Design and technology

Design and technology is possibly the curriculum subject for which English can give the widest range of genuine purposes to write. Every D&T project involves a series of steps from planning to evaluation, and each step produces a different type of writing. None of it is decorative. An incomplete plan leads to an incomplete outcome.

If English is the host subject, then biographical and explanatory writing are the strongest connections. Researching the work of an engineer or inventor and writing a mini-biography allows children to read several texts and synthesise the information, something required of them in the key stage 2 reading programme of study. Writing an explanation of how something works, such as a simple machine or structure, also repays investment. Explanation writing is one of the genres children get least practice in, and D&T gives the purpose to practise it. But when D&T is hosting, the writing is utilitarian and concise. Labels on a plan before building starts, or a written evaluation at the end of a project: in both cases, the writing has an immediate purpose. When it falls down, when the label is unclear or the evaluation imprecise, the pupil can see the results.

Art

Art and English work well together because so much children's reading matter is illustrated. Perhaps the relationship between the two is most active in picture books. Here, artwork is not illustrative; it exists as a second narrative running in parallel with the printed word. Pick up *Where the Wild Things Are* or *The Tiger Who Came to Tea* and ask pupils what the pictures are saying that the words aren't. You've got yourself a discussion about meaning that falls neatly into both disciplines.

If English is host, the natural links are made through close reading of illustration and illustrated writing of their own. Comparison of illustrations across editions of a picture book (consider how many versions of Little Red Riding Hood exist) teaches children about visual meaning. Asking older pupils to produce a double-page spread of their writing coupled with their own illustration, rather than simply handing in a neat sheet of prose, encourages consideration of layout and emphasis in a way that standard writing assignments do not. When art is host, children can practise English skills by interpreting what they see: describing a painting, discussing what it's about or writing a response to a sculpture.

Music

Music and English intersect most obviously in songs – because all songs have lyrics, and all lyrics are poetry. But the connection goes deeper: rhythm exists in language as well as music, and close listening is the same skill applied to different material.

When English is the host subject, the strongest link is poetry: reading song lyrics as poetry, both aloud and on the page, allows children to see how repetition and rhyme create meaning across a line break. Nursery rhymes fulfil this same function at key stage 1, embedding a pleasure in rhythm that will sustain them as readers for life.

Songs also provide mnemonic devices: a class that sings its spellings will remember them. Exploring oral storytelling traditions that stretch back millennia before writing reminds children that music and story were once one art form.

When music is the host subject, English lessons can focus on listening and responding. Writing a brief description in response to a piece of music, identifying what images or feelings the music brings, is descriptive writing with a particularly pure stimulus. Body percussion, used to accompany storytelling or poetry, can provide a doorway into rhythm for children who haven't discovered it through reading.

PE

PE may seem like the topic furthest away from English, but there are actually links more numerous than might at first appear. Children will write about what they're interested in, and many children are extremely interested in sport. When English is the host subject, sports fiction works well, but non-fiction is also powerful. Tom Palmer has written widely for primary-age children about football and other sports, and books by sportspeople such as Marcus Rashford bring younger readers inside sporting worlds in a voice they will trust. The *Little People, BIG DREAMS* series is another useful tool, with brief picture-book biographies of people from many spheres, including sport, that pupils can access at a key stage 1 reading level. Having children write a newspaper- or television-style report of their class sports day gives them a real purpose for wielding the conventions of sports reporting.

When PE is the host subject, the English work is focused on talk and description. Giving feedback to your classmates on their technique or explaining a rule to someone who doesn't know it both require the kind of precision described in the English programme of study. Dance can work too; a dance sequence inspired by and choreographed to represent a poem or Greek myth asks children to analyse a text with their bodies. That's close reading that doesn't involve a book at all.

In summary

The best cross-curricular links in primary English do genuine work for both subjects at once. They do not dilute the discrete teaching that each subject needs. Rather, they give children repeated, purposeful encounters with the language and texts they are being taught. The principles are the same across every subject. Start with a concept map. Pick one or two subjects as the main hosts of a theme. Work with other subject leads. Do not force links where none exists. Keep checking that both subjects are genuinely strengthened by the link, not just using each other as context.

Further reading

Andrews, J. and Jackson, C. (2018) 'Linking science and English for impact – developing standards of writing and science across the school', www.hfleducation.org/blog/linking-science-and-english-impact-developing-standards-writing-and-science-across-school

Beales, M. (2019) 'Top 10 tips for cross curricular links in English lessons', www.cambridge.org/it/education/blog/2019/05/21/top-10-tips-cross-curricular-links-english-lessons

Dalton, K. (2026) 'How cross-curricular learning can bring maths to life for primary school pupils', thirdspacelearning.com/blog/cross-curricular-learning-everyday-maths

Dolan, A.M. and Burns, I. (2016) 'Making connections with geo-literacy'. *Primary Geography*, (91), 18–19, https://portal.geography.org.uk/downloads/journals/PG_AUT_2016_DOLAN_BURNS.pdf

Science Fix (2021) 'Cross-curricular science: science and literacy', www.sciencefix.co.uk/2021/02/science-and-literacy

CHAPTER 12
FINAL REFLECTIONS ON PRIMARY ENGLISH

Primary English is made up of speaking and listening, reading and writing, but it is so much more. It is a functional skillset, yet also a fulfilling, empowering and enriching experience that allows children to make connections with each other and the wider world. The study of English gives children opportunities to express themselves, to build community and to understand each other, while growing in respect and compassion.

Teaching primary English is an incredible responsibility, pleasure and privilege. More than just teaching pupils how to spell or punctuate a sentence, it is the opportunity to guide them on a shared exploration of language, literature and, ultimately, society and culture. It is up to us to provide experiences in which children find joy in their learning, as well as a sense of achievement as confidence and independence grow. We help them to discover reading for pleasure and purpose, to develop empathy and to make connections. Through rich discussion, developing a love for books and helping children to express themselves through writing, teachers of English build meaningful shared experiences and provide children with a sense of belonging as the class embarks on a purposeful learning journey together.

Primary English is so complex and multifaceted that it feeds into every other subject area, drawing them all together. English often becomes one of the central points of a child's school experience. The vocabulary they develop helps them to understand science, history and maths. They are given the words to make sense of themselves and the world around them. Through exploration of authors' use of language, literary devices and the themes being shared, children are able to find meaning for their own lives that takes messages beyond what is written on the page and into their hearts and souls.

When considering how to deliver an effective programme of English, it is essential to remember that every setting, class and teacher is different. Factors such as school size, the structure of classes, resources available, access to a library or even access to internet all play a part in how the school will organise and plan. There is no one right way to teach primary English. Individual teachers must find the way forwards that works best for them and their setting, ensuring, first and foremost, that the needs of the children are met.

Primary English is a huge area of teaching and learning. It's impossible to implement or improve everything all at once, so it is important not to become overwhelmed by the task. Look for manageable, meaningful chunks. Consider the school development plan and your own priorities then create an achievable action plan and dive in.

Whether you are a new or recently qualified teacher just starting to create your ideal English provision, an experienced teacher wanting to make changes to a specific area of English or an English subject leader wanting to support and encourage others, I hope you discovered meaningful ideas and inspiration within these pages.

ACKNOWLEDGEMENTS

The Publishers would like to thank the following for permission to reproduce copyright material.

p.3 Quote from Beccy Earnshaw and Peter Hyman in *Oracy: the state of speaking in our schools*, by Millard, W. and Menzies, L. Voice 21, 2016. Reproduced by permission of Voice 21; **pp.6–7** Excerpt from *The national curriculum in England: framework document*, Department for Education, December 2014 (https://assets.publishing.service.gov.uk/media/5a7db9e9e5274a5eaea65f58/Master_final_national_curriculum_28_Nov.pdf)[1]; **p.19** Quote reproduced by permission of Veronica Price; **pp.20 & 40** Quote reproduced by permission of Richard Ruddick; **p.21** Quote reproduced by permission of Erin Hamilton; **p.22** Quote reproduced by permission of Sue Williamson/The Reading Agency; **p.23** Quote reproduced by permission of Sam Creighton; **p.24** Professor Teresa Cremin's 2019 reading for pleasure pedagogy research for The Open University, reproduced by permission of The Open University; **pp.34–5** Excerpt reproduced by permission of Dean Boddington; **p.35** Quote reproduced by permission of Jon Biddle; **p.39** Quote reproduced by permission of Cassie Hayward-Tapp; **p.40** Quote reproduced by permission of Alex Barton; **p.77** Quote reproduced by permission of Alex Galbraith/Farsley Farfield Primary School; **p.79** Quote reproduced by permission of Micaela Romero/Abbey Grange Church of England Academy; **p.82** Excerpt from EmpathyLab's website on Empathy Day vision (https://empathylab.uk/empathy-day). Reproduced by permission of EmpathyLab; **p.89** Quote reproduced by permission of Nicki Cleveland; **p.109** English curriculum map reproduced by permission of CLPE; **p.119** Excerpt from *Key stage 1 English reading test framework: national curriculum tests from 2016*, Department for Education 2015 (https://dera.ioe.ac.uk/id/eprint/23404/1/2016_KS1_Englishreading_framework_PDFA.pdf)[1]; **p.120** Excerpt from *Key stage 2 English reading test framework: national curriculum tests from 2016*, Department for Education, 2015 (https://assets.publishing.service.gov.uk/media/5a82454eed915d74e3402a2a/2016_KS2_Englishreading_framework_PDFA_V3.pdf)[1]; **pp.121–2** Quote reproduced by permission of Ashley Booth; **p.127** Quote reproduced by permission of Christopher Harrison/Oatlands Infant School; **pp.142–3** Excerpt from transcript of talk given at the Cambridge Assessment Network Conference, Faculty of Education, University of Cambridge, 15 September 2006, by Dylan Wiliam. Reproduced by permission of Dylan Wiliam.

[1] Contains public sector info licensed under the Open Government Licence v3.0. (https://www.nationalarchives.gov.uk/doc/open-government-licence/version/3/).

REFERENCES

Alber, R. (2011) '6 scaffolding strategies to use with your students'. Edutopia. Available at: www.edutopia.org/blog/scaffolding-lessons-six-strategies-rebecca-alber (accessed December 2023).

Anderson, L.W. and Krathwohl, D.R. (eds) (2001) *A Taxonomy for Learning, Teaching and Assessing: A Revision of Bloom's Taxonomy of Educational Outcomes: Complete Edition*. Longman.

Anderson, R.C., Wilson, P.T. and Fielding, L.G. (1988) 'Growth in reading and how children spend their time outside of school'. *Reading Research Quarterly*, 23(3), 285–303.

Andrews, J. and Jackson, C. (2018) 'Linking science and English for impact – developing standards of writing and science across the school'. HFL Education. Available at: www.hfleducation.org/blog/linking-science-and-english-impact-developing-standards-writing-and-science-across-school (accessed April 2026).

Ballin, B. (2019) Contributor in Willy, T. (ed.), *Leading Primary Geography*. Geographical Association.

Barton, A. (2023) Personal communication with author.

Beales, M. (2019) 'Top 10 tips for cross curricular links in English lessons'. Cambridge University Brighter Thinking Blog: English. Available at: www.cambridge.org/it/education/blog/2019/05/21/top-10-tips-cross-curricular-links-english-lessons (accessed December 2023).

Beck, I.L., McKeown, M.G. and Kucan, L. (2002) *Bringing Words to Life: Robust Vocabulary Instruction*. Guilford Publications.

Bichard, J. (2022). Peer recommendation bookmarks. Teachers' Reading Challenge. Available at https://cdn.ourfp.org/wp-content/uploads/2022 1115155920/Julia-Bichard-TRC.pdf (accessed May 2026).

Biddle, J. (2023) Personal communication with author.

Boddington, D. (2020) Reading for Pleasure Tube Maps. Available at: https://misterbodd.wordpress.com/2020/05/12/reading-for-pleasure-tube-maps-mkii-2020 (accessed April 2026).

Boddington, D. et al (2020) Books children should read in KS2 [Twitter comments on The Reading Agency post]. Available at https://x.com/readingagency/status/1686739048625233922 (accessed May 2026).

Booth, A. (2017) '100 book lists for primary classrooms'. The Teaching Booth. Available at: https://theteachingbooth.wordpress.com/2017/06/24/100-book-lists-for-primary-classroom (accessed April 2026).

Booth, A. (2020) 'A KS2 reading curriculum'. The Teaching Booth. Available at: https://theteachingbooth.wordpress.com/2020/06/28/a-ks2-reading-curriculum (accessed April 2026).

British Council, The Commonwealth and Voice 21 (2021) 'It's good to talk: oracy lesson plan'. Available at: www.britishcouncil.org/sites/default/files/its_good_to_talk.pdf (accessed April 2026).

Britton, J. (1970) *Language and Learning*. University of Miami Press.

Buczko, L. (2020) 'Making writing powerful: writing with purpose'. One Education. Available at: www.oneeducation.co.uk/making-writing-powerful-writing-with-purpose (accessed April 2026).

Cambridge Assessment International Education (2022) 'Education brief: oracy'. Cambridge University Press and Assessment. Available at: www.cambridgeinternational.org/Images/661428-education-brief-oracy-.pdf (accessed March 2025).

Clark, C. and Rumbold, K. (2006) 'Reading for pleasure: a research overview'. National Literacy Trust. Available at: https://nlt.hacdn.org/media/documents/Reading_for_pleasure_a_research_overview_2006.pdf (accessed April 2026).

Clark, C., Picton, I., Cole, A. and Bonafede, F. (2024) 'Children and young people's writing in 2024'. National Literacy Trust. Available at: https://nlt.hacdn.org/media/documents/Children_and_young_peoples_writing_in_2024.pdf (accessed April 2026).

Clements, J. (a) 'Let's not abandon text types: used creatively they can still support children'. Teachwire. Available at: www.teachwire.net/news/lets-not-abandon-text-types-used-creatively-they-can-still-support-children (accessed April 2026).

Clements, J. (b) 'Reading record – Download & alternative ideas for primary'. Teachwire. Available at: www.teachwire.net/teaching-resources/reading-records (accessed March 2024).

Clements, J. (2017) *Teaching English by the Book*. Routledge.

Centre for Literacy in Primary Education (CLPE) (2016) 'Choosing and using quality children's texts'. Available at: https://clpe.org.uk/research/choosing-and-using-quality-childrens-texts-what-we-know-works (accessed April 2026).

Centre for Literacy in Primary Education (CLPE) (2025) 'CLPE Reflecting Realities: survey of ethnic representation within UK children's literature, 8th edition'. Available at: https://clpe.org.uk/research/clpe-reflecting-realities-survey-ethnic-representation-within-uk-childrens-literature-3 (accessed April 2026).

Centre for Literacy in Primary Education (CLPE), English curriculum maps. Available at: https://clpe.org.uk/teaching-resources/english-curriculum-maps (accessed April 2026).

Centre for Literacy in Primary Education (CLPE) (2015–16) Reading and writing scales. Available at: https://clpe.org.uk/teaching-resources/reading-and-writing-scales (accessed May 2026).

Clarke, S. '5 steps for better peer marking'. Teachwire. Available at: www.teachwire.net/news/shirley-clarkes-fivesteps-to-better-peer-marking-in-the-primary-classroom (accessed April 2026).

Cleveland, N. (2024) Personal communication with author.

Corbett, P. (2008) *Good Writers*. National Strategies Primary.

Corbett, P. (2012) *Teaching English Creatively*. Talk for Writing.

Creighton, S. (2020) Twitter children's book community chat, 6 September.

Cremin, T. (2017) 'Motivating children to write with purpose and passion'. In Goodwin, P. (ed.) *The Literate Classroom* (4th edn). Routledge, pp.131–140.

Dalton, K. (2026) 'How cross-curricular learning can bring maths to life for primary school pupils' [blog post]. Third Space Learning. Available at: thirdspacelearning.com/blog/cross-curricular-learning-everyday-maths (accessed April 2026).

Department for Education (DfE) (2012) Research evidence on reading for pleasure. DFE-57519-2012. Available at: https://assets.publishing.service.gov.uk/media/5a7c18d540f0b61a825d66e9/reading_for_pleasure.pdf (accessed April 2026).

Department for Education (DfE) (2013a) English appendix 1: spelling. Available at: https://assets.publishing.service.gov.uk/media/5a7ccc06ed915d63cc65ce61/English_Appendix_1_-_Spelling.pdf (accessed April 2026).

Department for Education (DfE) (2013b) English programmes of study: key stages 1 and 2. National curriculum in England, September 2013. Available at: https://assets.publishing.service.gov.uk/government/uploads/system/uploads/attachment_data/file/335186/PRIMARY_national_curriculum_-_English_220714.pdf (accessed April 2026).

Department for Education (DfE) (2013c) The national curriculum in England: framework document. December 2014. DFE-00177-2013. Available at: https://assets.publishing.service.gov.uk/media/5a7db9e9e5274a5eaea65f58/Master_final_national_curriculum_28_Nov.pdf (accessed April 2026).

Department for Education (DfE) (2015a) 2016 key stage 1 English reading test framework: national curriculum tests from 2016. Electronic version product code: STA/15/7338/e ISBN: 978-1-78315-823-2. Available at: https://dera.ioe.ac.uk/id/eprint/23404/1/2016_KS1_Englishreading_framework_PDFA.pdf (accessed June 2026).

Department for Education (DfE) (2015b) 2016 key stage 2 English reading test framework: national curriculum tests from 2016. Electronic version product code: STA/15/7341/e ISBN: 978-1-78315-826-3. Available at: https://assets.publishing.service.gov.uk/media/5a82454eed915d74e3402a2a/2016_KS2_Englishreading_framework_PDFA_V3.pdf (accessed June 2026).

Department for Education (DfE) (2017) Teacher assessment frameworks at the end of key stage 1. Available at: www.gov.uk/government/publications/teacher-assessment-frameworks-at-the-end-of-key-stage-1 (accessed December 2023).

Department for Education (DfE) (2024) Early Years Foundation Stage (EYFS) statutory framework. Available at: www.gov.uk/government/publications/early-years-foundation-stage-framework--2 (accessed April 2026).

Department for Education and Skills (DfES) (2004) 'Speaking, listening and learning: working with children in key stages 1 and 2'. 0163-2004.

Diede, M. and Rigsby, K. (2021) '25 engaging lesson hooks'. Ditch That Textbook. Available at: https://ditchthattextbook.com/lesson-hooks (accessed April 2026).

Dolan, A.M. and Burns, I. (2016) 'Making connections with geo-literacy'. *Primary Geography*, (91), 18–19. Available at: https://portal.geography.org.uk/downloads/journals/PG_AUT_2016_DOLAN_BURNS.pdf (accessed April 2026).

Durran, J. (2019) 'Re-thinking "success criteria": a simple device to support pupils' writing' [blog post]. Available at: https://jamesdurran.blog/2019/01/24/re-thinking-success-criteria-a-simple-device-to-support-pupils-writing (accessed April 2026).

Early Career Hub (2020) 'Verbal feedback in primary English'. Available at: https://my.chartered.college/early-career-hub/verbal-feedback-in-primary-english/ (accessed December 2023).

Education Endowment Foundation (EEF) (a) 'Early Years toolkit: self-regulation strategies'. Available at: https://educationendowmentfoundation.org.uk/education-evidence/early-years-toolkit/self-regulation-strategies (accessed December 2023).

Education Endowment Foundation (EEF) (b) 'Teaching and learning toolkit: feedback'. Available at: https://educationendowmentfoundation.org.uk/education-evidence/teaching-learning-toolkit/feedback (accessed December 2023).

Education Endowment Foundation (EEF) (2020) 'Improving literacy in key stage 1'. Available at: https://educationendowmentfoundation.org.uk/education-evidence/guidance-reports/literacy-ks-1 (accessed April 2026).

Education Endowment Foundation (EEF) (2021) 'Improving literacy in key stage 2'. Available at: https://educationendowmentfoundation.org.uk/education-evidence/guidance-reports/literacy-ks2 (accessed April 2026).

Education Endowment Foundation (EEF) (2025) 'Phonics'. Available at: https://educationendowmentfoundation.org.uk/education-evidence/teaching-learning-toolkit/phonics (accessed December 2023).

EmpathyLab, Empathy Day. Available at: https://empathylab.uk/empathy-day (accessed December 2023).

Evans, S. (2023) *Reading for Pleasure: 100 Ideas for Primary Teachers*. Bloomsbury Publishing.

Gough, P.B. and Tunmer, W.E. (1986) 'Decoding, reading and reading disability'. *Remedial and Special Education*, 7(1), 6–10.

Green, S. (2021) 'Shining a spotlight on reading fluency'. Education Endowment Foundation. Available at: https://educationendowmentfoundation.org.uk/news/eef-blog-shining-a-spotlight-on-reading-fluency (accessed August 2023).

Hamilton, E. (2024) Personal communication with author.

Hayes, J. (2020) 'Working in pairs and groups'. Teaching English. Available at: www.teachingenglish.org.uk/teaching-resources/teaching-primary/activities/level-1/working-pairs-and-groups (accessed December 2023).

Hayward-Tapp, C. (2021) 'Let's talk books!' TES. Available at: www.tes.com/teaching-resource/let-s-talk-books-12564406 (accessed April 2026).

Heap, K. (2019) 'Learning Beyond the Classroom with Literacy Inspired Outdoor Education' Scope for Imagination. Available at: https://scopeforimagination.co.uk/2019/11/28/learning-beyond-the-classroom-with-literacy-inspired-outdoor-education (accessed April 2026).

Heap, K. (2020) *Developing Reading Comprehension Skills Years 5–6: Classic Children's Literature*. Brilliant Publications.

Heap, K. (2021) *Developing Reading Comprehension Skills Years 3–4: Classic Poetry*. Brilliant Publications.

Heap, K. (2022a) *Developing Reading Comprehension Skills Years 5–6: Contemporary Children's Literature*. Brilliant Publications.

Heap, K. (2022b) *Remarkable Ruby* by Terri Libenson. Guest post by Lucy (age 12). Scope for Imagination. Available at: https://scopeforimagination.co.uk/2022/10/25/remarkably-ruby-by-terri-libenson-guest-post-by-lucy-age-12 (accessed April 2026).

Iris Reading (2022) 'What is comprehension monitoring?' Available at: https://irisreading.com/what-is-comprehension-monitoring-explained-for-beginners/ (accessed January 2024).

Jago, A. (2021) 'Why I ditched the school spelling test'. *TES*. Available at: www.tes.com/magazine/teaching-learning/primary/why-i-ditched-school-spelling-test (accessed April 2026).

Khan, B. (2019) 'Tiered vocabulary: what is it and why does it matter?' Literacy in Focus. Available at: https://litinfocus.com/tiered-vocabulary-what-is-it-and-why-does-it-matter (accessed November 2023).

Learning by Questions (2023) 'Improve pupil progress'. LbQ Hub. Available at: www.lbq.org/hub/post/?posttitle=improve-pupil-progress-classroom (accessed December 2023).

Literacy with Miss P (2018a) 'Hosting a "book tasting"'. Available at: https://literacywithmissp.com/2018/06/08/hosting-a-book-tasting/comment-page-1/ (accessed April 2026).

Literacy with Miss P (2018b) 'Inspiring writing: publishing a book'. Available at: https://literacywithmissp.com/2018/07/27/inspiring-writing-publishing-a-book/ (accessed March 2024).

MacNeill, S. '5 ways to improve feedback in primary school'. Teachwire. Available at: www.teachwire.net/news/5-ways-to-improve-feedback-in-primary-school (accessed December 2023).

Millard, W. and Menzies, L. (2016) 'Oracy: the state of speaking in our schools'. Voice 21. Available at: https://voice21.org/wp-content/uploads/2019/10/Voice-21-State-of-speaking-in-our-schools.pdf (accessed May 2026).

Moorhead, J. (2021) 'Keep parents out of it: the expert who wants schools to give up weekly spelling tests'. *The Guardian*. Available at: www.theguardian.com/education/2021/jul/03/jane-considine-spelling-test-reading-primary-school (accessed February 2024).

Mrs P Teach (2021) 'How to plan reading lessons'. Available at: www.mrspteach.com/2021/03/how-to-plan-reading-lessons.html (accessed December 2023).

Mullis, I.V.S., Martin, M.O., Kennedy, A.M. and Foy, P. (2007) 'PIRLS 2006 International Report', chapter 4, p.146. Available at http://timss.bc.edu/PDF/P06_IR_Ch4.pdf (accessed April 2026).

NATE Primary Matters (2020) *The Teaching Sequence for Writing*. National Association for the Teaching of English.

National Literacy Trust (2013) 'A guide to text types: narrative, non-fiction and poetry'. Available at: www.thomastallisschool.com/uploads/2/2/8/7/2287089/guide_to_text_types_final-1.pdf (accessed April 2026).

National Literacy Trust (2023) 'Children and young people's writing in 2023'. Available at: https://literacytrust.org.uk/research-services/research-reports/children-and-young-peoples-writing-in-2023/ (accessed October 2023).

National Literacy Trust (2024) 'Children and young people's writing in 2024'. Available at: https://literacytrust.org.uk/research-services/research-reports/children-and-young-peoples-writing-in-2024/ (accessed March 2024).

Open University (a) 'Active reading: critical reading techniques'. Available at: https://help.open.ac.uk/critical-reading-techniques/active-reading (accessed July 2023).

Open University (b) 'Reading for Pleasure'. Available at: https://ourfp.org/reading-for-pleasure-pedagogy/ (accessed July 2023).

Open University (c) 'Teachers' knowledge of children's literature and other texts'. Available at: https://ourfp.org/finding/teachers-knowledge-of-childrens-literature-and-other-texts/ (accessed April 2026).

Oracy All-Party Parliamentary Group (2021) 'Speak for Change'. Available at: www.education-uk.org/documents/pdfs/2021-appg-oracy.pdf (accessed July 2023).

Organisation for Economic Co-operation and Development (OECD) (2023) 'PISA 2022 results (Volume I and II) – country notes: United Kingdom'. Available at: www.oecd.org/en/publications/pisa-2022-results-volume-i-and-ii-country-notes_ed6fbcc5-en/united-kingdom_9c15db47-en.html (accessed April 2026).

Palmer, S. (2006) *The Complete Skeleton Book for Non-fiction Text Types*. TTS Skeleton.

Palmer, S. (2016) 'Skeletons for Organising Writing' [video]. Oxford Education. Available at: www.youtube.com/watch?v=PGkKEq3QnJM (accessed April 2026).

Palmer, S. and Corbett, P. (2003) *Skeleton Poster Books for Writing Genres* [six books]. TTS Skeleton.

Peat, A. (2008) *Writing Exciting Sentences*. Creative Educational Press Limited.

Pennac, D. and Blake, Q. (2006) *The Rights of the Reader*. Walker Books.

Pimley, G. (2011) 'Making cross curricular links'. *Teach Primary Magazine*. Available at: www.teachprimary.com/learning_resources/view/making-cross-curricular-links (accessed December 2023).

Price, V. (2023) Personal communication with author.

PRIDE Reading Program (2023) 'How to teach visualizing and improve reading comprehension'. Available at: https://pridereadingprogram.com/how-to-teach-visualizing-and-improve-reading-comprehension/ (accessed January 2024).

Putman, R. (2017) 'Using research to make informed decisions about the spelling curriculum'. *Texas Journal of Literacy Education*, 5(1), 24–32.

Rasinski, T. (2022) 'Why focus on reading fluency?' Education Endowment Foundation. Available at: https://educationendowmentfoundation.org.uk/news/why-focus-on-reading-fluency (accessed April 2026).

Rasinski, T. and Padak, N. (2012) 'Vocabulary: five common misconceptions'. Available at: www.ascd.org/el/articles/vocabulary-five-common-misconceptions (accessed November 2023).

Reading Agency, The (2024) 'Reading facts'. Available at: https://readingagency.org.uk/our-work/our-research/reading-facts/ (accessed July 2023 and new website in March 2024).

Reading Agency, The, 'Running a poetry slam'.

Reading Rockets (2026a) Classroom strategy library. Available at: www.readingrockets.org/strategies (accessed July 2023).

Reading Rockets (2026b) Choral reading. Available at: www.readingrockets.org/strategies/choral_reading (accessed July 2023).

Reading Rockets (2026c) Reciprocal teaching. Available at: www.readingrockets.org/classroom/classroom-strategies/reciprocal-teaching (accessed July 2023).

Rippel, M. (2009) 'Effective spelling strategies'. *All About Spelling* series. Available at: https://creation.com/en/articles/effective-spelling-strategies (accessed May 2026).

Rockin Resources (2014) 'Writing mini lesson #9: the writing process'. Available at: https://rockinresources.com/2014/11/writing-mini-lesson-9-the-writing-process.html (accessed April 2026).

Rockin Resources (2015) 'Writing mini lesson #24: revising a narrative essay – delete'. Available at: https://rockinresources.com/2015/06/writing-mini-lesson-24-revising.html (accessed April 2026).

Ruddick, R., *They Don't Count as Reading* [blog]. Available at: https://comicsinclass.school.blog (accessed April 2026).

Ruddick, R. (2023) Personal communication with author.

Said, S.F. (2003) *Varjak Paw*. Illustrated by Dave McKean. David Fickling Books.

Said, S.F. (2013) *Phoenix*. Illustrated by Dave McKean. David Fickling Books.

Said, S.F. (2017) 'Three steps to writing' [blog post]. Available at: www.sfsaid.com/2017/01/three-steps-to-writing.html (accessed April 2026).

Said, S.F. (2024) 'The writing of *Varjak Paw*' [blog post]. Available at: www.sfsaid.com/2024/06/ (accessed April 2026).

Samuels, S.J. (1979) 'The method of repeated readings'. *The Reading Teacher*, 32(4), 403–408.

Science Fix (2021) 'Cross-curricular science: science and literacy'. Available at: www.sciencefix.co.uk/2021/02/science-and-literacy (accessed April 2026).

Sedita, J. (2023) 'Question generation: a key comprehension strategy'. Reading Rockets. Available at: www.readingrockets.org/topics/comprehension/articles/question-generation-key-comprehension-strategy (accessed January 2024).

Sensible Senco (2026) PIVATS: performance indicators for valued assessment and targeted learning, 5th edn. Available at: www.sensiblesenco.org.uk/pivats (accessed April 2026).

Shanahan, T. (2017) 'Everything you wanted to know about repeated reading' [blog post]. Available at: www.readingrockets.org/blogs/shanahan-literacy/everything-you-wanted-know-about-repeated-reading (accessed July 2023).

Sherrington, T. (2017) *The Learning Rainforest: Great Teaching in Real Classrooms*. John Catt Educational.

Sherrington, T. and Caviglioli, O. (2020) *Teaching Walkthrus*. John Catt Educational.

Sims Bishop, R. (1990) 'Mirrors, windows, and sliding glass doors'. Originally published in *Perspectives: Choosing and Using Books in the Classroom*, 6(3), Summer. Available at: https://scenicregional.org/wp-content/uploads/2017/08/Mirrors-Windows-and-Sliding-Glass-Doors.pdf (accessed April 2026).

Spell Wizards, 'Spelling tests: are they effective?' Available at: https://spellwizards.co.uk/are-spelling-tests-effective (accessed April 2026).

Spence, G. (2021) 'Whole class reading – support for all'. *Primary English*. Available at: https://primaryenglished.co.uk/blog/whole-class-reading-support-for-all (accessed April 2023).

Stirling, J.A., How to teach kids about writer's voice'. The Children's Book Review. Available at: www.thechildrensbookreview.com/how-to-teach-kids-about-writers-voice (accessed May 2024).

Temple Learning Academy, 'Oracy'. Available at: www.templelearningacademy.org/learning-at-tla/primary-specific/oracy/ (accessed April 2026).

Tidd, M. (2013) 'Why is mastery just for maths?' [blog post]. Available at: https://michaelt1979.wordpress.com/2013/10/18/why-is-mastery-just-for-maths/ (accessed April 2026).

Tidd, M. (2014) 'A mastery model for writing: moving away from the text type treadmill' [blog post]. Available at: https://michaelt1979.wordpress.com/2014/06/30/a-mastery-model-for-writing-moving-away-from-the-text-type-treadmill/ (accessed April 2026).

Tidd, M. (2016) 'Writing for a purpose (or 4!)' [blog post]. Available at: https://michaelt1979.wordpress.com/2016/08/29/writing-for-a-purpose-or-4/ (accessed April 2026).

Tiffany, S. (2023) *Mr T Does Primary History*. Corwin UK.

UK Literacy Association (UKLA), 'UKLA Viewpoints: Assessing English'. Available at: https://ukla.org/ukla_resources/ukla-viewpoints-assessing-english/ (accessed April 2026).

Voice 21, 'What is oracy?' Available at: https://voice21.org/what-is-oracy/ (accessed April 2026).

Voice 21 and Oracy Cambridge (2020) 'The Oracy Framework'. Available at: https://membership-hub.voice21.org/the-oracy-framework (accessed April 2026).

Wiliam, D. (2006) Transcript of talk given at the Cambridge Assessment Network Conference, Faculty of Education, University of Cambridge, 15 September.

Williamson, S. (2023) The Reading Agency, video published on X, 2 August. Available at https://x.com/readingagency/status/1686739048625233922 (accessed April 2026).

Wilson, R., 'What is Big Writing?' Andrell Education. Available at: www.andrelleducation.com/big-writing (accessed November 2023).

Writing for Pleasure Centre (2022) 'The components of an effective writing lesson'. Available at: https://writing4pleasure.com/2022/07/22/the-components-of-an-effective-writing-lesson/ (accessed April 2026).

Young, R. (2019) 'What is it Writing for Pleasure teachers do that makes the difference?' The Goldsmiths' Company & the University of Sussex: UK [online] Available at: https://writing4pleasure.com/what-is-it-writing-for-pleasure-teachers-do-that-makes-the-difference-research-report/ (accessed July 2023).

Young, R. (2021) 'A writing for pleasure manifesto'. The Writing for Pleasure Centre. Available at: https://writing4pleasure.com/wp-content/uploads/2020/12/new-writing-for-pleasure-manifesto-.pdf (accessed April 2026).

Zutell, J. and Rasinski, T.V. (1991) 'Training teachers to attend to their students' oral reading fluency'. *Theory Into Practice*, 30, 211–217.